Hollywood Diary

A Work of Non-Fiction by Richard Lamparski

Author of the eleven volume *Whatever Became of...?* series and

Hidden Hollywood: Where the Stars Lived, Loved & Died

and *Manhattan Diary*

Hollywood Diary

Twelve Untold Tales of

Gary Cooper   Patsy Kelly   Pola Negri

Robert Taylor   Zeppo Marx

The Grapes of Wrath   A Star Is Born

"Our Gang"   Rock Hudson   Soupy Sales

Quentin Crisp   Mae West

Over 40 Illustrations

A Work of Non-Fiction by

Richard Lamparski
Author of the Whatever Became of...? books

BearManor Media
2006

Hollywood Diary: Twelve Untold Tales of Gary Cooper,
Patsy Kelly, Pola Negri, Robert Taylor, Zeppo Marx, Quentin Crisp,
The Grapes of Wrath, *A Star Is Born*, "Our Gang," Rock Hudson,
Soupy Sales, and Mae West

© 2006 Richard Lamparski

All rights reserved.

For information, address:

BearManor Media
P. O. Box 750
Boalsburg, PA 16827

bearmanormedia.com

Cover design by John Teehan

Typesetting and layout by John Teehan

Published in the USA by BearManor Media

ISBN—1-59393-052-6

for

SHIFRA HARAN

1913 - 1987

My oldest friend and the youngest

person I've ever known

Table of Contents

Acknowledgements i

The Hollywood Fans All Over the World Dream Of 1

Darla Was a Darling 25

One of Hollywood's Little People 37

The Absolute Worst Story I Know 51

The Queen of Sex 57

A Rainy Afternoon in Beverly Hills 71

Lassie's Master 83

A Star Is Born 91

A True Hollywood Romance 97

Up and Coming 115

Whoever Heard of Jean Malin? 123

My All-Time Favorite Hollywood Story 147

Index 163

Acknowledgements

Melanie Adler, Paul Gilbert Adrian, Chris Albertson, Steven Bach, Don Bachardy, Jerry Bauer, Beverly Hills Historical Society (Martin Geimer), Bob Board, Nick Bougas, Sherry Britton, Shelly Brodsky, Frank Buxton, Dick Bann, Eddie Brandt's Saturday Matinee, Bill Cappello, Diana Serra Cary, John Cocchi, Kirk Crivello, Dale Crawford, Columbia Pictures, Critt Davis, David Del Valle, Tim Doherty, Joe Franklin, Michael Fitzgerald, James Gavin, Jeff Gordon, Hal Gefsky, Diana Hall, Howard W. Hays, Jeff Hanna, Curtis Harrington, Charles Higham, Michael R. Hawks, J. J. Johnston, Marty Jackson, Sybil Jason, Jim Kotsilibas-Davis, Michael Knowles, Kurt Kreuger, Don Koll, Brooke Kroeger, Joel Lobenthal, Harry Locke, Jack Larson, Gavin Lambert, Eileen Lottman, Jimmy Lydon, Lon "Bud" McCallister, Mike Marx, Michael Monroe, Byron Matson (Merle Norman Collection), MGM, Lawrence Orme, Diedre Owens, Paramount Pictures, Public libraries of Academy of Motion Picture Arts & Sciences, Beverly Hills, California, Santa Barbara, California, San Diego, California, Museum of the City of New York, Thousand Oaks, California, Detroit, Michigan, Santa Monica, Jordan Ringel, Jaime Rigler (Arts Channel), Richard Schaeffer, Peter Schaeffer, Raymond Schwede, Ken Sephton, John Scarry, PhD., Schomburg Center for Black Culture, Bob Satterfield (Sons of the Desert), Soupy Sales, Tony Slide, David Sten, Twentieth Century-Fox Corp., Bart Williams, Marc Wanamaker (Bison Archives), Warner Bros., Ken Warfield, Lou Valentino, United Artists.

The Hollywood Fans All Over the World Dream Of

When one evening in 1975 Chris Albertson, the jazz critic and biographer of Bessie Smith, phoned me from New York to carry on about a film, *The Naked Civil Servant*, which he had just viewed over PBS, I surprised him by recognizing the name of its central figure, Quentin Crisp.

"I might know I couldn't tell you about a demented queen you'd never heard of," he replied feigning annoyance.

During the early sixties I was seeing a lot of Emlyn Williams, especially while he was appearing on Broadway in *Daughter of Silence* ('61). I took the actor-playwright to tea one Sunday afternoon at the apartment of John Noble, a recent immigrant from England who was about to be appointed curator of miniature furniture at the Museum of the City of New York*. Emlyn became intrigued upon learning that Noble's live-in lover was an ordained priest of the Polish National Catholic Church**, and he was very keen on seeing the couple's collection of pornography.

A framed head-shot arrested his interest as soon as Fr. Bobby had taken his hat and coat. It was of John Noble taken by England's preeminent theatrical portrait photographer of the period, Angus Mc Bean. In it, our host sported lacquered fingernails, the length and sheen of those worn by the Sax Rohmer villain Fu Manchu. His eyelashes appeared beaded, and he affected a Joan Crawford by Hurrell pose and mood.

Emlyn, arched an eyebrow and asked, 'So, you're one of *those*, are you?"

---

* From 1961 to 1985 John Noble was the curator of toys at the Museum of the City of New York.
** The Polish National Catholic Church is described in the New Catholic Encyclopedia as the "Only permanent schismatic sect from American Roman Catholicism." The church was formed near the turn of the twentieth century and had over 272,000 members as of May, 2001.

Quentin Crisp, author, actor, wit. 1908-1999.

Neither the Polish padre, who was American, nor I realized that he had immediately identified John as one of the young homosexuals who hung around Quentin Crisp of Nottinghill Gate. They copied the eccentric's flamboyant style, a mute protest against machismo and conformity. It was then I first learned of the Crisp cult and that he was as well known to Londoners as "Broadway Rose*" and "Moondog**" were to New Yorkers.

John, who had considerably modified his look as he neared forty and sought U.S. citizenship, talked for sometime about the liberating influence Crisp had had on him and the other acolytes.

It had remained vivid in my mind because Noble gave me an inscribed copy of the McBean picture after he was made to realize the hopelessness of his crush on me. To put him off, I claimed to be attracted only to adolescents. On the 8x10 he wrote: "Wishing I were 16 again…"

On the day after New Year's, 1980, I took myself to the desert for a bit of sun, an interview, and to visit with Patsy Ruth Miller, Lon Chaney's Esmeralda in *The Hunchback of Notre Dame* ('23). We had remained in close touch since she became one of the first to appear on my radio program in 1965. When she mentioned to Ruth Taylor that I was coming down, both of us were invited for lunch.

Our hostess, "Lorelei Lee" in the silent version of *Gentlemen Prefer Blondes* ('28), had retired from the screen after marrying a wealthy stockbroker, now deceased.

Older ladies who were once beautiful and celebrated and who are

---

* "Broadway Rose," as she was dubbed by habitués of the Great White Way, was to be found nightly during the 50's and 60's preaching the gospel to onlookers, usually at the southwest corner of 43 St. She held a bible in one hand and the pole bearing a large U.S. flag in the other.

** Louis Hardin, who composed music and poetry under the name "Moondog", lost his eyesight in an explosion when he was 16 years old. In 1979, *The New York Times* referred to him as a "New York living landmark for thirty years."

now merely well dressed and rich do not wish to know from Jeeps. Even clean, pretty, air-conditioned ones. I, therefore, drove Pat's Cadillac from Palm Desert, where she lived to the very smart Le Vallauris in the Springs.

The fourth member of our party was Ruth Taylor's houseguest, also a widow. "Foxie" something or other.

Luncheon was alfresco under the azure blue skies in a part of the resort in which everyone and everything one sees absolutely smacks of money.

As the drinks were being served, our hostess got it in, as she did any time I'd ever been with her, that her son was Buck Henry. At that time there was no one in the film capital more "in," socially and career-wise. This was the cue for someone, anyone there, to say how effective he was playing the father in Milos Forman's *Taking Off* ('71) or that as co-author of the original screenplay for *The Graduate* ('67) he shared an Oscar nomination with Calder Willingham. Either or both remarks would have triggered Ruth Taylor to explain that he was actually a hyphenate. That was the current term being used in Hollywood for those who do more than one thing. Henry did three. He also directed Warren Beatty in the hit film *Heaven Can't Wait* ('78).

Her three guests were well aware of Buck Henry as was anyone who knew his mother. Her routine on that occasion was for the benefit of the waiter. Now he, too, knew.

The "Foxie" lady on my left and I both ordered the lobster salad. That done, she fixed her slightly watery eyes on me over the salty rim of her marguerita glass and said, "My son was born the same year as Ruth's. When I became pregnant, I went to Evangeline Adams for a reading. Do you know who she was?"

I knew that during the twenties, she was the equivalent of what Carol Righter had since become, the astrologer to celebrities. They both told the stars what their stars had in store for them.

Evangeline Adams had predicted correctly that the child she was carrying would be her only one and that it would be a boy.

"Then, Mr. Lamparski, she added something that well…" said my luncheon companion with years of practice. "She said that he would be either a genius…or a criminal."

"And he is…?" asked I as I was expected and supposed to.

"My son," said the proud mother beaming triumphantly, "is…Stephen Sondheim."

I had breakfast the next day at The Pantry, a restaurant that had somehow managed to retain a menu and atmosphere that strongly suggested a 1940's time warp.

Most of that afternoon was spent with the musician-comedian Phil Harris, who, with Alice Faye, comprised one of those couples touted as among one of the "most happily married" in the entertainment capital.

I had expected to meet with Harris where I had been told he and his wife lived, on the green at the Thunderbird Country Club. Instead I was given directions to another residence facing the golf course at the Ironwood Country Club. His explanation was that it had been left to him by Bing Crosby, his best friend. Harris said he used it as his office. I thought it more likely that after thirty-nine years of marriage, the Harrises were living apart. My suspicions were confirmed when one of the former sidemen from his band who was watching TV in one of the bedrooms answered the phone and then called in, "It's Alice, Phil. She's making pork chops for supper. We're invited. Wadda ya say?"

Harris said "Yes."

Over the almost twenty years as a regular cast member of Jack Benny's radio show and six years co-starring with his wife on their own network series, Phil Harris had established a public image as a lush. During that time, drunkenness, even alcoholism, was considered a fit subject for comedy on the air as on the stage and screen.

Throughout our time together, Harris sat at the bar in his den and sipped an amber liquid from a Picardie glass.

When I took out my camera, he freshened his drink and then lined up several bottles of liquor by his elbow and made with the celebrity smile. When I paused to slip in another film cartridge, he said, "I've always refused to endorse any particular brand of booze. Wouldn't want to slight the others. They're all just great!"

That struck me as hopelessly, pathetically dated thinking. In his heyday, which had ended about twenty years before, we were told musicians played better and writers did their best work after drinking heavily. They told this to themselves, to each other and to their public. There were even people who maintained they drove better when drunk.

Phil Harris knew the title and format of my books. He knew what he had said and exactly the impression the photograph would make. I mentioned as I was packing up that I intended to use his quote as a caption to the picture. This meant his reputation would again be confirmed, and his big florid face beamed approval.

I grew up half a block from the Irish bar owned by my maternal uncle. From early childhood I was in it a lot. He and both of his brothers were alcoholics. All my life I've known some serious drinkers. I think what Phil Harris drank throughout that afternoon was apple juice on the rocks. To my senses, he spoke and moved and smelled like someone who had been on the wagon for a very long time.

I was free to be away overnight from my home in the Hollywood foothills and my St. Bernard, Baby Dumpling, because one of my neighbors, the actor Frank Christi was usually available and more than willing to look after her. Even if he was appearing, as he did semi-regularly, on such shows as *Kojak* or *Baretta*, he was able to come home on his lunch hour for her mid-day walk because the private road we lived on, Carse Drive, was only a few minutes away by car from Universal and Warner Brothers studios.

Frank was known professionally for playing tough guys. Off the screen he was one, the son of a Sicilian labor organizer from Brooklyn. In social situations he came off as a flashily dressed hoodlum who for that particular moment was behaving himself. His longtime girl friend, Margie Lanier, was a dead-ringer for the bug-eyed, bubble-headed, gold-digging chorus girls Richard Taylor used to draw for *The New Yorker* and *Esquire* in the forties and fifties. As a couple they looked like they stepped out of the cast of *Guys and Dolls*.

Anyone who has spent much time around the Copacabaña in New York or the Crescendo on the Sunset Strip knew Christi's type, which was usually referred to as a "Nightclub Wop." There was also a Jewish variety called a "shtarker." They were there to keep an eye on the bartender, handle anyone who got out of line and threaten all the right people.

Frank's reward for being such a good neighbor during that trip was being taken to see *An Evening with Quentin Crisp*. We had enjoyed *The Naked Civil Servant* together on TV and his one-man show was every bit as intelligent and entertaining.

After the performance as we drove to Trumps for a late supper, I told him that I intended to send Quentin Crisp a copy of my most recent book along with a note. I would offer him a personally guided tour from the research I had been doing for my next book, *Lamparski's Hidden Hollywood, Where the Stars Lived, Loved and Died*.

When our drinks were placed before us, he raised his and said, "This is to you and Crisp. You *deserve* each other."

One midnight three years later Frank Christi was murdered by gunmen in his carport. The crime has never been solved.

The day after I left the book and invitation with the concierge at the Beverly-Wilshire Hotel, a message of acceptance was left on my answering machine: "I should like nothing better than to be shown Lamparski's Hollywood by the man himself. I'm free all day on the twenty-fourth. That's a Thursday. I can be reached at..."

Crisp and I spoke briefly to set the time I would fetch him at the entrance to his hotel.

When I pulled up, he was chatting with the doorman who appeared oblivious that the elderly gentleman was wearing violet eye shadow or that he had a lavender rinse of his long white hair which was tucked under a trilby hat. All this at 10:30 in the morning.

Crisp was turned westward on the look-out for my Jeep. His opening line was to thank me for describing my car as having a yellow body and white top, "I saw you blocks away. It looks just as you said it would, like a large lemon meringue tart."

When I told him that was how Anne Shirley had once described it, he exclaimed, "*Anne Shirley! Anne of Green Gables, Stella Dallas* and Mrs.

The Grosvenor apartment at the corner of South Rodeo Drive and Charleville Boulevard in Beverly Hills was the residence of many screen personalities.

This building, which is no longer standing, on South Rodeo Drive was once the famous Hollywood eatery, Romanoff's.

John Payne. My grand tour has already begun!"

When we spoke over the phone, he gave me a few names of his ultimate screen favorites, all from the twenties and thirties. If it was agreeable to him, I would not give him even a hint of what he was about to experience.

"I give myself over to you, Mr. Lamparski, with complete trust and as much innocence as I'm able to muster," was his commitment.

I circled around the hotel to point out the Grosvenor at the corner of Charleville Boulevard and Rodeo Dr. In the fifties I had heard that Joan Crawford owned it. I knew she kept an apartment there. At the time the word around was that it was so her children wouldn't be exposed to her lovers.

The facade of the structure at 140 S. Rodeo Dr., except for the sign proclaiming it a Chinese restaurant, looked exactly as it did for all the years it was the famed Romanoff's, hang-out of "Bogie", Sinatra, Clark Gable and other such swells of filmdom.

Using the brochure "Trips to the Homes of Movie Stars" Richfield Oil service stations dispensed in 1932 to motorists, we drove by the former home of Zeppo Marx at 518 No. Rodeo Dr. Up two blocks was where two-time* Academy Award winner Fredric March and his wife Florence

---

* In 1931-32 he and Wallace Beery tied as Best Actor, March for his performance in *Dr. Jekyll and Mr. Hyde*. In 1946 he won in the same category for his role in *The Best Years of Our Lives*.

Eldridge once lived.

My guest was over twenty years my senior. Before anyone coined the expression "The Movie Generation," he was a member of it. He shared my fascination with the personalities of the screen and gave a knowing roll of his eyes when I pointed out 728 Rodeo Dr. as where Gary Cooper was living during his Lupe Velez period. The "Mexican Spitfire" dwelled two doors south.

"Who says nobody *walks* in Hollywood?" Quentin Crisp wondered.

Because *Freaks* ('32) is one of my all-time favorite films, I was especially pleased to show him 808 No. Rodeo. Dr., where Todd Browning was living while he directed it.

"*Freaks* is near the top of your list, is it?" said my passenger. "I'm in even better hands than I had thought."

At Sunset Blvd. I stopped to phone the butler at Pickfair, as Buddy Rogers had asked me to do. The gates of the estate at 1143 Summit Dr. were open during the daylight hours, but anyone driving through set off an alarm in the servants' quarters. Alerted, he turned it off for a few minutes allowing us to proceed up the driveway and through the portico that had sheltered the entrances and exits of the King and Queen of Siam, England's Edward VII when he was the Prince of Wales and, of course, Rudolph Valentino.

That name invoked, we proceeded to 1436 Bella Dr., the last home of the screen legend.

On our way I drove up the brick roadway of 1085 Summit Dr. around the three-tiered planter in the large courtyard and out again. The interior decorator of the current owner, George Hamilton, had secured permission for me to give Crisp a glimpse of where Charlie Chaplin had spent most of his years in the film capital. It was where he had brought his brides, Lita Grey, Paulette Goddard, Oona O'Neill, and where he had lived with Joan Barry, who bore what she maintained, and what the courts of California had concurred, to be his child.

The hillside estate of the great Latin lover of silent pictures is mostly hidden from the road behind a high wall, but by peeping through the space between the gates Crisp could get a good look at the large forecourt. The big thrill was seeing the name "Falcon Lair" in raised letters at the top of the pillars on both sides of the entryway. But he also loved hearing that another of his idols, Pola Negri, had lived there for a while during World

War II and that the current owner was Doris Duke*, reputedly the wealthiest woman in the world.

I went by the faux Mayan residence of the southeast corner of Sunset Blvd. and Roxbury Dr., number 822, so he could see where Marlene Dietrich had lived while making *Morocco* ('30) and *Blonde Venus* ('32).

On the eastside of No. Linden Dr., I pointed out 724 as where Irving Thalberg, MGM production head from its formation in 1924, lived with his wife, Oscar-winner** Norma Shearer. Down a few doors at 718 was the abode of the screen smoothie Edmund Lowe, who was married to the actress billed as the "Best Dressed Woman in the Movies," Lilyan Tashman until her death in 1934. Errol Flynn and Lily Damita lived in marital discord in 701. I paused before 604 so he could ogle the former home of Lon Chaney, "The Man of a Thousand Faces."

I entered the semi-circular driveway at 1100 Lexington Rd. at one end and drove out the other opening to show my guest the mansion Columbia Pictures founder, Harry Cohn, bought from Marion Davies. It was there in 1926 that silent star Eleanor Boardman married King Vidor, who directed her, most notably opposite James Murray in *The Crowd* ('28). John F. Kennedy, then a congressman, and his bride Jackie spent part of their honeymoon there in 1953. I had recently taken tea with its present owner and her houseguest, Helen Mack, star of *Son of Kong* ('33).

We lunched at Oscar's Wine Bar across Sunset Blvd. from the Chateau Marmont Hotel. The small restaurant drew many celebrities, but could accommodate those who did not wish to be seen in its room in the rear. Those seeking attention, and Quentin Crisp admittedly loved it, were displayed in one of several booths just inside the front door.

Oscar's owners, a pair of youngish Londoners, were delighted to have us there and went out of their way to make the quiet sort of fuss the English do so well. Between courses, both the chef and his assistant came to our table separately to pay homage to their esteemed countryman, extolling him in the thick brogue known as "Liverpool Irish."

Italy's Vittorio Gassman smiled as he bowed on his way out. Producer Allan Carr gushed about Crisp's show after our hosts introduced him. He then sent over a very nice bottle of Australian white. As it was being uncorked, Quentin Crisp allowed that the highlight of our morning had been for him cruising by 704 No. Palm Dr. where Ruth

---

* Doris Duke died in Falcon Lair in 1993.
** Norma Shearer received the 1929-'30 Best Actress Academy Award for her role in *The Divorcee*.

Chatterton* had lived during her divorce from Ralph Forbes and her marriage to George Brent. The industry was in the throes of the hurried transition to sound, and with an Oscar nomination and several smash hits in a row, she was riding the crest of the craze in the early thirties for what was called "Women's pictures." She is best known, however, for her final film, *Dodsworth* ('36).

The toast we drank was to her, Ruth Chatterton "The First Lady of the Talkies."

As my companion was finishing his crème brulée, I declared that we had seen sufficient of the city's sunny side. The rest of our day would be spent amidst Hollywood's darker fringes, both living and dead, my specialty.

I took him to 856 Holloway Dr. and then behind the shabby apartment house to the garages where in 1976 Sal Mineo was stabbed to death. A quiet smile told me my passenger especially like the turn our tour was taking.

His success late in life had brought Quentin Crisp the celebrity he had longed for without daring to hope for. It had earned him money, which after sixty some years of poverty, he could not bring himself to spend. It had, also, made possible his move from England to the U.S. After having been shunned from childhood, he had been taken up by fashionable people.

Fame had come his way due to a change in the times, but his maturity was also a major factor. An *old* painted queen is not perceived as a threat.

Although Crisp and I were of different generations, nationalities, and styles, we had other, far more important, things in common. Neither of us had ever been in love with anyone and felt none the worse for it. Like me, he held no loyalties to family or country. Like him, I acknowledged no "best friend." Our favorite company was our own. We were readers and observers and prized above all things our privacy and individuality.

At one point I allowed that with all the dues he and paid and the lumps he had taken, any minority group other than homosexuals would have elevated Quentin Crisp into something akin to sainthood. His silent response would have played beautifully on stage or screen. He leaned forward slightly so that he could study my expression without blocking my view of traffic. There was a rueful smirk on his face.

What Crisp projected so skillfully said it all. I had been fully aware of the irony in my remark. Both of us knew all too well that among homosexuals there are no heroes, only heroines. Males are revered chiefly

---

* Ruth Chatterton was nominated as the Best Actress of 1929-'30 for *Sarah and Son*.

as sex objects. The others are all simply competition, friendly and otherwise.

I took him by the soundstages that were once Columbia Pictures and 870 Gower St. with its three steps that had led to the front door of R-K-O and later Desilu Studios. We then saw the gates of Paramount Pictures that swung open for Gloria Swanson's Isotta-Fraschini with Erich Von Stroheim* at the wheel in *Sunset Boulevard* ('50).

We could have walked to our next destination, 6326 Lexington Ave. The four story Warner-Kelton Hotel was built there in the late twenties, just off Vine St., with walking in mind. Its guests were mostly the Broadway crowd, performers and writers who came out from the East with a one-picture contract or merely a hope to "break into the movies," as it was called within their profession.

The hotel's co-owner, was Pert Kelton, who had worked in vaudeville from childhood. The act she did with her parents concluded with the pert Pert doing a full split without missing a note on her cornet. Jackie Gleason fans remembered her as the original "Alice Kramden" of *The Honeymooners*.

The trouper knew what show people were looking for in the way of accommodations and conveniences. Her hotel was on a quiet street in a respectable neighborhood near bus and streetcar lines.

For a while Pert Kelton had been a comic foil to the master of comedic timing, the fabled Frank Fay. Likewise the comedienne Patsy Kelly, who lived at the hotel on and off for years.

The Warner-Kelton was costume designer Orry-Kelly's first home in

The screenwriter/film historian DeWitt Bodeen remembered seeing Katharine Hepburn seated on the stairs to her studio reading her fan mail shortly after the release of her auspicious screen debut in *A Bill of Divorcement* (1932).

---

* The vehicle had to be towed because Von Stroheim did not know how to drive.

Paramount Pictures.

his adoptive country after he and the acrobatic dancer, Archie Leach, arrived in Hollywood in 1931.

The latter sometimes wandered by after a day's work at Paramount, where he had been renamed Cary Grant.

Evenings were *the* time to be around Pert's place because that is when you could watch what the residents had been up to during the day. At the rear of the hotel was a small outdoor theatre. The big doors at the back of its stage opened onto an alley for quick and easy changes of scenery. During daylight hours, this area bustled with performers trying out new routines or rehearsing and polishing their acts. On warm nights they performed under the stars for the fellow residents, friends in the business, agents and directors. Some did what they did best, were known for doing. Others showed-off new stuff, material no one had seen before. It was part audition and part party, because in the basement of the Warner-Kelton was a speakeasy.

When we turned to leave, I mentioned that, although there was no record of the song-writing team Richard Rodgers and Lorenz Hart having stayed there, they were working in the early thirties at Paramount only a few blocks away. They *must* have known about it, Pert Kelton's *small hotel**.

"And there it is…," Crisp all but gasped, indicating the wishing well to the left of the back door.

The Warner-Kelton was the residence of some who were trying to re-invent themselves, and/or make a come-back, such as Al "Fuzzy" St. John. After working as second banana to Buster Keaton, Roscoe "Fatty" Arbuckle and, in *Tillie's Punctured Romance* ('14), Charlie Chaplin, he had a long second career in sound pictures as sidekick to cowboy stars Jack Randall, Larry "Buster" Crabbe and Bob Steele. In most of the Lash La Rue oaters, St. John provided the comic relief.

Pert Kelton, circa 1934.

It was also home to those thought to be "all washed up" in pictures. One of them was Raymond Hatton, who had been featured prominently in early Cecil B. De Mille productions and later in comedies with Wallace Beery. During the thirties, he was a supporting player in Johnny Mack Brown and Buck Jones westerns.

Hatton, and those like him, didn't need to explain to the hotel's manager what their names had once meant on movie theatre marquees. He was Monroe Salisbury whose acting career went back to Cecil B. De Mille's *The Squaw Man* ('14).

I told all of this to Crisp while we passed through the lobby of what by then, 1980, had become a residence for those on welfare.

Because I felt the words of greeting in raised letters at the entryway would have more meaning for Quentin Crisp after he knew the building's history, I waited until we exited.

From the sidewalk in front I pointed back to the inscription in relief over the front door: "Joyously Enter Here."

---

* Richard Rodgers and Lorenz Hart respectively wrote the music and lyrics of "There's a Small Hotel" for the show *Jumbo*, but it was not heard until a year later in *On Your Toes* ('36).

The Keltons built a full-size stage among the bungalows behind the main building. Paul Gilbert Adrian photo.

The Warner-Kelton Hotel, some believe, was the inspiration for the song that is now considered a standard, "There's a Small Hotel (with a wishing well"). Paul Gilbert Adrian photo.

We walked past my car to the corner of Vine St., where I bade him look across to what was a TV studio. When it opened in 1926 as the La Mirada Theatre, it featured a huge Wurlitzer organ that accompanied the silent features on its screen. After that art form had been replaced by talkies, its name was changed to the Filmarte. The new policy was the exhibition of foreign made movies interspersed with occasional great hits from the pre-sound era. De Witt Bodeen, scenarist and Hollywood historian, grew up in Los Angeles during the golden age of silent pictures and as a college boy frequently attended the Filmarte, often with his teenage sister, Karen. He had told me of seeing not only the features from the past, but the players in them who came to see their work of years before at these showings.

It was easy to imagine those living at the Warner-Kelton walking the few yards to the corner and crossing Vine St. to watch themselves in their salad days.

Bodeen told me of one night as he and his sister were exiting the Filmarte's lobby after seeing a re-release of Murnau's silent masterpiece *Sunrise* ('27). They heard someone from behind him cry out "George O'Brien!"

"A few yards ahead of us the man we'd just seen playing opposite Janey Gaynor, spun around, burst into a big movie star smile and called back 'In Person!'"

Rogers and Hart were working only a few blocks away from the Warner-Kelton Hotel at Paramount Pictures just before their song "There's a Small Hotel" was introduced in the Broadway musical, On Your Toes (1936).

"O'Brien was with his Mrs., and sometime leading Marguerite Churchill," explained DeWitt. "The guy who recognized him was the west-

The Warner-Kelton Hotel.

ern star of silents and talkies, Hoot Gibson*. Everyone, even the boy behind the candy counter, began applauding them. The O'Briens and Gibsons, went off together in one car to C. C. Brown's up on Hollywood Blvd., for hot fudge sundaes, I suppose. Karen and I would have followed them, but it was a school night. Hoot's wife, Sally Eilers, was driving, by the way. Only in Hollywood."

All of this I related to Crisp as we drove a few blocks east to Barton Ave.

I could have prepared my guest for our next stop by describing the interior of the house we were about to visit at the rear of 6026. It looked as though Jean Cocteau was sharing digs with the Collyer** brothers. I might have mentioned that the person he was about to meet, Samson De Brier, was as well known in Hollywood as Crisp was in London and that he was a longtime friend of Kenneth Anger. The auteur of the film *Fireworks* ('47) and author of *Hollywood Babylon* rented the ground floor of the building at the front of the lot. Not only had De Brier's tenant boarded over the windows, he painted both the walls and ceilings of one of the rooms with black lacquer. Instead, I led Crisp through the little gate, down the driveway and past a lattice-work door that opened onto the junk-filled yard of Samson De Brier, diarist, miser and saloniste.

I saved this for the end of our tour because our host was known to take a siesta each afternoon. As the celebrity biographer George Eells said, "Samson climbs in on the dot of three and doesn't open the coffin's lid till the stroke of five." Part of De Brier's reputation throughout Hollywood was that he was a warlock.

He liked people just dropping by so long as it wasn't before noon or during his nap. It was 5:15. His door was ajar. I knocked. No answer. After a minute or so I called inside, "Samson!" and knocked again. Silence.

The third time I pounded on the side of the frame cottage and all but screamed, "Samson! You have visitors."

---

* Hoot Gibson is rated as #17 on Boyd Magers list of the "Top 100 Cowboys of the Century."
** The story of the brothers Collyer, descendants of one of New York's oldest families, made front pages across the U.S. in the spring of 1947 when the eldest, Homer was found dead in their once luxurious mansion at 128 St. and Fifth Ave. At the times of their births, 1881 and 1885, Harlem was a very fashionable address. It took two weeks of digging through newspapers and periodicals dating back prior to World War I before the body of Langley Collyer, partially devoured by rats, was discovered under some of the 136 tons of things that were eventually removed from the three-story building. Among the debris were: over 3000 books, a Steinway piano, guns and ammunition, a kerosene stove, gas chandeliers, an X-ray machine from around the turn of the century, the chassis of an old car, human medical specimens, a saw horse, the folding top of a horse drawn carriage and a horse's jawbone.

Often residents of the Warner-Kelton would stroll around the corner to the Filmarte Theatre at 1228 North Vine Street. It was only a 900 seat neighborhood house but the Filmarte was beautifully appointed with all the extravagances of the day.

Still no response. I knew he was about or the door wouldn't be open. The waiting was awkward, but I didn't know what else to do.

Another long pause ended when Crisp exclaimed from behind, "He's *dead*. It's the start of a thriller!"

Seconds later the door swung open and a kimono-clad Samson De Brier appeared before us. Immediately spotting Crisp over my shoulder, he greeted

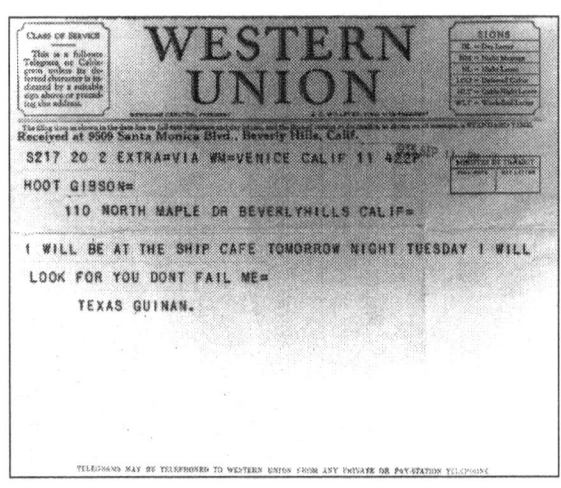

Hoot Gibson is rated second only to Tom Mix as the most popular western star of the era of silent films. In September, 1933, when Texas Guinan, whose unofficial title was "Queen of the Speakeasies," wired him to meet her at the Ship Café, he was in the process of being divorced from his former leading lady, Sally Eilers, who was by then a star in her own right.

him with "At last we meet. I must tell you how sick I am of being asked if I'm Quentin Crisp."

I made my way to the bathroom while the septuagenarians settled themselves in the musty, dusty parlour, Samson at his little desk alongside the photograph of himself swathed in a fur-collared coat with matching cap. It was from his Parisian period, the mid-twenties, when he was taking tea with Gertrude Stein and Alice B. Toklas and getting blow-jobs on an irregular basis from Andre Gide.

By leaving the door open while I peed, I could hear their talk getting underway with Crisp's opening remark. After carefully moving the antique dolls on the tattered velvet loveseat into a cluster, he sat down amidst the faded, chipped and tarnished faux grandeur of another time and said, "Your abode is the most delightful dé ja vu for me, Mr. De Brier. I see that you, too, have learned the wisdom of simply not bothering."

One of Crisp's lines in his one-man show was that after a couple of years of neglect, homes were arrested somehow at a certain level of messiness and remained in that state indefinitely. As he put it: "By then one has grown quite used to it. After all, it's your own dirt."

I left the two of them and went shopping a few blocks away at the Hollywood Ranch market. I reckoned that by the time I returned they would have gotten each other's numbers in both senses of the expression. Just as I suspected, they got on beautifully. Samson had invited him to a brunch on the following Sunday at the art nouveau house of movie director Curtis Harrington*.

In the Hollywood Memorial Park Cemetery I took him to corridor "C" in the Cathedral Mausoleum, which holds the casket and remains of Rudolph Valentino and around the corner to #308, the last resting place of his contemporary Barbara LaMarr, the "Girl Who Was *Too* Beautiful." There were flowers in the vases alongside both. Our next stop was Peter Lorre's ashes which were in a small urn at the building's other end in #5, Tier I. The character actor was one of my guest's favorites for his performances in the screen classis *M* ('31), *The Man Who Knew Too Much* ('34), *The Maltese Falcon* ('41) and *Casablanca* ('42).

From there we went directly across the roadway to the graves of Nelson Eddy and his mother, side by side and then around to the sarcophagus of Harry "King Cohn" Cohn that looms over the simple marker of his brother Jack. A few yards away, just beyond the Tyrone Power me-

---

* Best known for having directed *Night Tide* ('63) and *What's the Matter with Helen?* ('71).

morial that closely resembles a marble bus bench, is a mausoleum marked "Douras," the original family name of Marion Davies.

In her time she had been one of the most popular and publicized of the early screen stars. She died in 1961, one of the wealthiest. Through her close relationship with media magnate William Randolph Hearst, she was arguably, the most influential woman in Hollywood. What so fascinated me about Marion Davies was that she did not appear to draw envy or antagonism. Not one of the countless people I had met who knew her both slightly and well told me anything other than about her warmth and generosity and of what fun she was to be with.

We stood at the steps leading to the tomb's massive bronze doors as I repeated to Crisp my favorite compliment paid to a movie star. It was uttered by Tennessee Williams following his first meeting with Marion Davies: "She makes up for the rest of Hollywood."

Then we proceeded northward along the shore of the lagoon to see the bronze marker reading "Virginia Rappe 1895-1921," the so-called victim in the Roscoe "Fatty" Arbuckle case, one of filmdom's most sensational scandals. Although ruined professionally, the great comic was eventually cleared of all charges.

On our way to the Abbey of the Psalms on the Gower St. side of the graveyard, I pointed out the sarcophagi of Adolphe Menjou and Cecil B. De Mille.

The grave of Tyrone Power is only a few years from the mausoleum of Marion Davies.

Natalie Talmadge was the eldest of the three Talmadge sisters, a star of dramatic features and the wife of movie mogul Joseph Schenck, and actor George Jessel.

Constance Talmadge was a leading comedienne of the silent era. She never appeared in talkies.

Crisp had been one of the many millions of fans of Norma and Constance Talmadge during their period of worldwide popularity in the twenties. They were interred along with their mother and sister Natalie, who had been married to Buster Keaton, near one of the Abbey's entryways.

While he gazed at the Talmadge family crypt of rose marble complete with its own stained glass window, I proceeded into the adjoining Abbey of the Sanctuary of Light, where my friend Darla Hood the "Sweetheart of *Our Gang (Little Rascals)* had been laid to rest, high up near the ceiling of the main room in space #7213.

Anyone who knew the name Clifton Webb from his days as an arch and dapper song-and-dance man on Broadway and/or his screen roles in *Laura* ('44), *The Razor's Edge* ('46) and the "Mr. Belvedere" series was aware of his devotion to his mother, Maybelle. They had lived together from his birth until the octogenarian died in 1960 when her son was seventy-one years old.

When I pointed out the bronze plaques engraved "Clifton Webb 1891-1966" at #2350, next to the niche bearing the inscription "Maybelle Webb 1869-1960" Crisp murmured sardonically, "Touching."

On one of my many visits to that cemetery over the years I had come across a crypt in the Abbey of the Psalms that I showed to Quentin Crisp just before we left. "My," he said, 'I shouldn't have wished to go through life with that name." The plaque is engraved: "GAY CRUM".

There was just enough time and it was on our way back to Beverly Hills, so I cruised by 172 No. McCadden Pl., where the Hudson sisters lived in *Whatever Happened to Baby Jane* ('62). Since it looked as though no one was home, I took my passenger up the driveway so he could get a close look at the iron gates against which, in the film, Jane Hudson (Bette Davis) is supposed to have crushed her older sister Blanche (Joan Crawford) with their Duesenberg, thereby crippling her for life.

The three Talmadge sisters are entombed along with their mother in the rose marble crypt of the Abbey of the Sanctuary of Light in Hollywood Memorial Park Cemetery. Paul Gilbert Adrian photo.

As we passed the venerable Ristorante Chianti on Melrose Avenue Crisp remarked that on the previous Sunday evening he had dined there in a banquette across from Mr. and Mrs. Gregory Peck. In that case, I thought he would enjoy knowing that it was W. C. Field's favorite place for Italian cuisine. I knew this from the great comedian's longtime companion Carlotta Monti, author of *W. C. Fields and Me*.

"Had I only known," he replied. "The food would have tasted even more delicious." Then he recalled laughing even on his way to London cinemas to see such Fields starrers as *It's A Gift* ('34) and *The Man on the Flying Trapeze* ('35).

With that I turned left at the first light and took Beverly Boulevard west. Just before Doheny we pulled into the rear area of another of the city's longest established restaurants, Chasen's. All I told my passenger was that it was the favorite of former California governor Ronald Reagan who was

The home of Blanche and Baby Jane Hudson, 172 No. McCadden Place. Paul Gilbert Adrian photo.

about to challenge President Jimmy Carter in the upcoming presidential elections. I had Crisp wait in the car while I went inside and upstairs to the office of its owner, Maud Chasen. I had recently secured her permission to reproduce a John Decker painting in the calendar I was planning to produce. Mrs. Chasen had seen *The Naked Civil Servant* and was delighted to show the portrait to my guest, but without a word as to its subject.

Courtesy of Chasen's.

The proprietress led us through the large bustling kitchen and then into the main room where busboys and bartenders were preparing for that evening's customers. The work of art hung in the vestibule to the right of the entrance. He had known the camp masterpiece existed, but never imagined that he would see the original, his favorite funnyman, W. C. Fields in drag as Queen Victoria.

I never saw Quentin Crisp again, but we stayed in touch through mutual acquaintances and the mail. I still cherish what he gave my publisher as a blurb for a dust jacket of one of my volumes of *Whatever Became of...?* "I opened this book expecting much bitchiness and found it to contain not one speck."

If there was a single moment that I would have liked to have been in his company it was in the late nineties at the end of an encounter with one of his neighbors in the East Village. The other man, Lester Glassner is a person of such acquisitiveness that his four story brownstone had been described as "Impossible to imagine beforehand or exaggerate after seeing. Make that 'experiencing'."

His original plan was that all of the tens of thousands of things he had acquired would eventually comprise a museum. His would be the first and only display of everything that had been sold in that once great American institution the 5¢ and 10¢ store. Throughout much of my lifetime there was one in every neighborhood and in the smallest of towns. They were patronized by every age and social strata. Diana Vreeland, "The Empress of Fashion" used to ask underlings whenever an item needed for a photo shoot or display had not yet been found, "Has any one of you tried the dime store?"

The collector of dimery memorabilia had recently been persuaded by either his lawyer or CPA against opening a museum when Quentin Crisp accepted an offer to be shown through his house at 64 East 7 St. I had known Lester for years through the tough-talking blonde of the screen, Iris Adrian, who was featured on the cover and throughout his book *Dime Store Days* ('81). He had stayed in my home in the Hollywood Hills. Much of this man's fifty-some years as well as a great deal of money had been spent collecting. He was well known for what he owned. He was that guy with the huge showcases lining every room and reaching almost to the ceilings of his turn-of-the-century building. Each and every cabinet was chock-full of what dime stores had sold during the thirties into the fifties, which was just about everything. His professional reputation was based on what he owned. His social life revolved around it. It was, in his mind, what and who he was, the "King of the 5¢ and 10¢ stores."

When the grand tour concluded, Glassner walked Crisp back to the rooming house where he made his home at 46 East 3 St.

I never learned what Glassner said that brought on the remark Crisp made. He was at this point well into his eighties and had just had a generous Scotch on the rocks. Perhaps along the way Lester asked why Crisp chose to live in a single room, preparing his meals on a hot plate and sharing a bath down the hall with several others? He wrote books and a regular column and had recently appeared in a feature film.* A very comfortable apartment was well within his means.

Quentin Crisp's parting words to Lester Glassner on that day were: "You are owned by your possessions. Sell every one of them. Give them away. Destroy them all. Get yourself free."

From the moment Quentin Crisp climbed into my vehicle that morning until I dropped him off at the Beverly-Wilshire, he held himself so that his face was turned toward me. At first I thought it was a form of courtesy, looking directly at his host instead of the road ahead. I intuited, however, as the day wore on and I found him throughout either facing me or at my rear that positioning himself in these ways was part of his general strategy as he went through life. Having been reviled, bullied and beaten since childhood, he was always on guard to ward off yet another attack. Almost all of his seventy-two years had been lived on the defensive.

Never before nor since those eight hours or so Quentin Crisp and I were together have I attempted to entertain anyone who appeared so attentive and appreciative. I felt he saw every detail, heard every word and picked up on every implication.

After stepping out of my vehicle in the hotel's porte cochere he turned back toward me. His thanks and farewell were spoken through the window: "On this day, Mr. Lamparski, you have shown me the Hollywood fans the world over *dream of!*"

---

* Quentin Crisp played England's Queen Elizabeth I in *Orlando* ('92)

Darla Was a Darling

June 15, 1979, was what in our house we called "Fried Piggy Day." Every four or five weeks we had one, but this day, a Friday, was a particularly full one. On the following Monday morning I was scheduled to fly to Fort Wayne, Indiana, to give a lecture. Jean-Louis D'Heilly, who since joining the executive staff of the University of Oriental Studies, had asked to be addressed as "Kailasadhamma," would be staying with Baby Dumpling while I was gone. I wanted to leave a good size supply of her favorite treat, crisp bacon. This meant I had to get her out of the house while the "piggy" was being fried as the smell of it cooking sent her wild with anticipation and it lingered for hours. Having stopped eating red meat shortly before the St. Bernard came into my life didn't prevent me from feeding it to her, but I hadn't liked the odor of pork even when I ate it.

By ten o'clock, I had breakfasted, and we had had our morning walk. I then dropped her off with Jean and Jeanette, a mother and daughter team who bathed and groomed dogs in their Burbank home. This time she was to be "dipped", as they called it, for fleas. During hot weather, it was necessary at least once a month because of all the fleas and ticks that thrived in the wooded hills where we lived. By eleven I had fried the piggy and locked the house up tight after it and our Jeep had been thoroughly sprayed with the chemical used by the exterminator. It had to be left that way for a minimum of four hours. A faint odor lingered for the remainder of the day and evening, thus effectively killing whatever was left of the bacon smell.

From 2 until 4 PM I viewed the Faberge exhibit at the Los Angeles County Museum with my very stylish chum Sara Richardson, recently of the Stuttgart Ballet. She had returned to the U.S. to be near her widowed father who was in poor health and her older brother who was awaiting a suitable donor to replace his heart.

After the exhibition, Sarah gave me tea in her cottage in the Normandie Towers, a group of quaint semi-detached buildings in the 7200 block of Hampton Ave. in West Hollywood. It was built during the twenties with minarets, cupolas, spires and a dry-but-dear little wishing well complete with bucket. Rumplestiltskin, Rapunzel, and the Seven Dwarfs would all have looked right at home there. Her landlord had claimed the complex was built by Charlie Chaplin, whose studios were only a few blocks away on La Brea Ave. Their storybook styles were somewhat similar. I, however, had written to the great comedic actor when I was researching my book *Lamparski's Hidden Hollywood* and was promptly informed by his secretary on Manoir de Ban letterhead that "Sir Charles" had no knowledge of Normandie Towers.

Sarah drove me back to Carse Dr. We needed the Jeep to fetch Ms. Dumpling.

My stock reply to "Do you live in Hollywood?" was always that I was "In it, but not of it." Hopefully, none of those I said that to saw the three of us returning home on that early evening. I had brought with me one of the many big kerchiefs I had for my pet. As I looked in the rearview mirror, there was her huge head sticking out the window behind me. Around her neck was a deep purple cotton square flapping in the breeze. People honked and smiled and waved at the guy in the big shades driving along with the babe in even bigger ones and wearing a silk turban.

Sarah had dined the night before with a member of her former dance company. He gave her some Thai stick which we were both looking forward to smoking. As we came down the driveway into my dell it was almost seven o'clock, which meant it was time for a drink.

My guest was approximately fifteen years my junior and had been living mostly in Europe for the past decade. She wasn't very familiar with movies of the past or the personalities I wrote about. Still, she could see from the expression on my face as I heard the words emanating from my telephone answering machine that someone I and the caller felt close to was dead.

Sybil Jason had phoned to tell me before I heard on the news that Darla Hood had died suddenly hours before. "The Sweetheart of Our Gang" had been in the office of her physician awaiting an examination when she fell over dead from heart failure. It was a brief message because the Warner Brothers kid star of the thirties was so choked up.

Sarah and I had our dope and drinks on the porch, which was the last place I had seen Darla. I had come home one day that spring to find

From left to right (back row) Joe Besser, Mathew "Stymie" Beard, Arthur "Dagwood" Lake, Ray Stricklyn, Tommy Rettig. (Front row) Irish "Sheena, Queen of the Jungle" McCalla, Richard Lamparski, and Darla Hood.

her sitting with her stockinged feet on the coffee table gazing at the gurgling fountain in the center of the yard. After an appointment at one of the nearby studios, she had bought a cold bottle of soda at the Liquor Locker at the foot of the street leading to Carse Dr. My neighbor, Frank Christi, was there with Baby Dumpling and Darla recognized her. She asked if I was home because she didn't have my unlisted number with her and wanted to stop by. Knowing I was due within half an hour, Frank suggested she wait on my porch where she could listen to KUSC through the screened windows and sip her drink.

She was returning from a casting office, where instead of having her read for a part, she was introduced to everyone, it seemed, at the studio, including a boy from the mailroom. Once again she had been induced to get herself up and drive through the smog and traffic, by the vague mention of a "network commercial for a major brand."

"It's the slow season," Darla explained. "Someone in the department must have come across my picture in the Academy Players Directory. Why not find out how she looks these days? It would make them appear busy and, who knows maybe there was a big shot who had a crush on me as a kid. Someone made points, getting me there, so someone else could meet me."

Still, Darla went that day, as she always had. In that business, if they call, you go.

I knew who Darla Hood was even before I was old enough to go to first grade. My mother used to take my to Friday matinees at Detroit's Cinderella Theatre held for preschoolers. Every week they showed one of the series of shorts my generation knew as *Our Gang*. They had achieved an even greater popularity on television under the title *Little Rascals*. As soon as I mentioned the series to Sarah she said, "Of course, Darla with the little panties showing."

I first saw her in person when she appeared in Ken Murray's *Blackouts*. Darla was one of the early guests on my radio show. It was through me she and Buckwheat got back in touch after over twenty years. Often when I was asked by those booking television talk shows to recommend guests from my books, I suggested her. Sometimes I appeared on panels with her and two or three of her contemporaries.

After I told Sarah how Darla Hood was another example of a child being used by her parents for their own gain, we drank to her.

Then, by way of illustrating the kind of person she was, as well as the quality of the life she had been let to live, I repeated what she revealed to me ten years before in Cincinnati.

Dennis Wholey, my fellow Detroiter and WBAI alumnus, had his own talk show televised over WKRC-TV, a station owned by the Taft Broadcasting Company. At my suggestion Darla had been brought from New York, where we were both then living, to guest. For the appearances we were each paid AFTRA minimum, and all of our expenses were picked up. I got to plug my books, and she was given exposure on television.

I was always happy to accept an invitation to Dennis's show because Cincinnati had two excellent, if very pricey, restaurants. I always had a Lucullan meal at one of them.

On the flight there, I described the décor and the cuisine at each. Darla immediately chose the Gourmet Room, which was on the roof of the Hilton Hotel where we were staying, although I hadn't told her its location. When we entered the lobby and she saw there was an express elevator to it, she said something about being glad it was "Right here." It was a mild night and the other option, the Maisonette, was also downtown. We weren't due at the studio until noon the next day. I didn't understand why, but she was clearly relieved.

Darla beamed as the maitre d' seated us alongside one of the huge windows affording a panoramic view of the city. Because, she said, it was such a special occasion she, too, would have a cocktail before dinner. I took this to mean she seldom drank.

When I requested the wine list, Darla grew absolutely pale and said, "Richard, do you really think we should? Wine *and* two drinks?"

My companion was not worried about either of us drinking too much. She was seriously concerned that we would be running up too high a bill.

"Darla," I tried to explain. "When I go to a really fine restaurant, I put cost out of my mind. It's not conducive to a good appetite. Anyway, this is on the filthy rich Taft family. The one Senator Robert Taft was from. What does their money matter to us?"

But it mattered very much to Darla Hood. That's why she chose the Gourmet Room, because it sounded less expensive. That was why she was relieved it was in our hotel. It meant we wouldn't have to take taxis. The prices on the a la carte menu caused her grave concern. You weren't supposed to cost producers a lot of money. That was what her mother had instilled in her since she first went under contract to Hal Roach at the age of four. All the other "Gang" members had been told the same. They talked about it among themselves when they were on publicity tours.

Between 1936 and 1945 Darla Hood acted in over one hundred and fifty *Our Gang* comedies. For those nine years she thought she was living the same kind of life as most children her age. She was an only child and all the others she came in contact with, which is to say the only others she knew, had publicists and tutors and directors. They were all in the movies. Not that she had many friends among them. The girls all had other scripts to memorize and other schedules on other sets or lots. The boys in *Our_Gang* were nice to her, but being a girl, she wasn't invited to join them when they had free time.

By the late thirties when production of *Our Gang* was taken over by MGM, Darla was old enough to seek out playmates. By wandering around the lot, she met Elizabeth Taylor. They were best friends until the studio declined to pick up the option on the services of the fourteen year-old Darla.

My companion saved the orange slice from her whiskey sour for next to the last. Just before placing it into her mouth she said, "Let's live it up, Richard." There was a touch of abandonment in her voice. As though to say, "After they get the bill for all this, neither one of us will ever be asked back, anyway."

Darla mentioned that occasion many times over the years. It was the first time she ate cherries jubilee and when they were flambéed she exclaimed, "Richard, this is just like in the movies."

The next day on the flight home I heard about an incident from her childhood that I might have told at her wake or funeral, had I been able to attend either. In her fall from the examining table, Darla's forehead had struck the floor with great force. It took the undertakers a full day to reduce the swelling and disguise the bruise. I would be out of state both Monday and Tuesday. My only chance to say good-bye was late Sunday afternoon, the earliest her remains would be available for viewing.

What Darla told me was of one of her walks around the Metro lot with her favorite doll, looking for someone to play with. Just when it became apparent there were no other little girls around, live music drew her onto a soundstage where Artie Shaw and his orchestra were rehearsing a number for *Dancing Co-ed* ('39), which would star MGM's sex kitten Lana Turner. Shaw's recording of "Begin the Beguine" was a smash hit, and *Downbeat* magazine had just proclaimed that he, not Benny Goodman, was now the "King of Swing."

Artie Shaw had star status as well as being quite good-looking.

The eight-year-old Darla Hood knew better than to draw attention to herself. She wasn't even sure she was allowed to be there. Standing in the shadows, she watched as Lana Turner entered and walked toward the bandstand. Shaw was facing his musicians and couldn't see her, but within seconds was aware that someone or thing of great interest was approaching behind him from the eyes of the men he was leading.

The "Sweater Girl," as she was then being publicized, was on this day wearing tight white shorts and two bandanas tied into a halter.

The leader came down from the podium and there was a brief, private exchange that concluded when Lana Turner stood on her tip toes, tilted her head upward and closed her eyes. Shaw bent slightly and kissed her. As he did so, he ran his left hand appreciatively, slowly, over her ass.

Then she turned away and sashayed across the vast floor and out. The only sounds were of sandals flapping. With the thump of the quilted door, Lana Turner and her ass were gone.

Artie Shaw, who had been as transfixed as his men, raised his left palm and touched it to his outstretched tongue. The "Tsish!" the drum-

When Lana Turner starred in Marriage is a Private Affair *(1944), she had already married and divorced Artie Shaw, the first of her eventual seven husbands.*

mer made with his brushes resounded throughout the huge soundstage followed by hoots, hollers, and a sprinkling of applause.

Darla knew she had witnessed something, but she wasn't sure what.

"I was puzzled, but not upset," she told me thirty years after the incident. "It was my first lesson in boy-girl stuff."

A few months later, Lana Turner and Artie Shaw eloped.

I never heard Darla complain about her past or present, but when interviewers asked about residuals for the many movie shorts that were then being seen around the country, on literally hundreds of televisions stations, she made it clear that she got none. As to the money she made as a child actress, her parents never gave her a cent of it.

After her father, a bank clerk, died Mrs. Hood remarried. It must have been her stepfather I spoke with briefly at Pierce Brothers Mortuary on that Sunday afternoon.

The mortician who ushered me into a small chapel where Darla was lying in state told me I would be the first to see her and to sign the registry. The room was empty except for the floral tributes and her coffin, which was on a low stage.

I was raised Roman Catholic, and had been seeing corpses since ever I can remember. As a small child during the thirties I was taken to view neighbors and relatives who were then usually laid out in their own homes. About the time of the U.S.'s entry into World War II, even working class people began being buried from funeral parlours. As an altar boy I saw several serviceman killed in action whose caskets remained closed. They were, however, opened just before burial when the priest gave them the final blessing with holy water while I perfumed the air with incense as I swung the censer behind him.

I have always welcomed the opportunity of seeing someone I cared about one last time. It helps to bring closure and it reminds me of my own mortality, especially when, as in this case, the deceased is only forty-eight, my senior by less than a year.

I stood looking onto the lifeless figure surrounded in ruffled satin with very mixed feelings. Sadly, this was the only time I had seen Darla Hood that she didn't look cute or pretty, and she was both until the day she died.

Probably to hide the damage to her head, she was wearing a wig. It wasn't a very good one, and it didn't look like her own hair. On the other hand, the faint suggestion of sad resignation I had always sensed in her, was completely absent.

Whatever one's beliefs, the phrase "At rest" gives great comfort.

After a bit, I took a seat in the front pew and pondered some of the laughs we had over the years we had known each other. I remembered how surprised and delighted Darla was when at a book signing in Farmer's Market Mathew "Stymie" Beard, whom she had not seen in over twenty years, came in wearing his trademark derby hat.

At another such get-together, this one held in the Brentano's in the Beverly Wilshire Hotel, Darla sat between Jack "The Merchant of Menace" La Rue and Virginia O'Brien who carried a large pocketbook on which someone had embroidered caricatures of herself doing her famous dead-pan stare. Tommy Rettig and Sunset Carson, in his full cowboy regalia complete with chaps and ten-gallon hat, received fans at the other end of the long table.

Darla had seen all of the "Baby Sandy" features when she was a child and was looking forward to meeting the star that day. She kept a perfectly straight face throughout, but exclaimed as soon as we left, "Richard, I expected her to have grown, but really!"

"*IMMENSE*," is all I said and we both convulsed on Rodeo Drive.

That afternoon's highlight came when one of the bookstore's clerks discreetly made me aware of the small, dark man who seemed to be browsing across from the long table where the personalities were seated. Dustin Hoffman is much more believable when he is acting than when he is pretending. There was no subtlety in the way the Oscar-winner studied all five of my guests as they related to their fans.

The last time we were together in a professional situation was at the May Co., which proved to be one of the most successful promotions in that branch's history. The store's security had to put up ropes to hold back the hundreds who came out on that afternoon to meet Joe Besser, once one of the "Three Stooges," "Stymie," Darla, Ray Stricklyn, Tommy Rettig, Irish "Queen of the Jungle" McCalla, Arthur "Dagwood" Lake, and Lauren "Father Knows Best" Chapin.

Each received a real ovation as he or she was introduced. They then signed copies of my book, autographs, stills and posed for pictures. But, as it is at a movie premiere, it is the hardcore Hollywood buffs who dominate such crowds, and it is they who decide who is the ultimate star on each given occasion.

On that day once the personalities got down to the business of signing and such, everyone there, including the host, saw their thunder of minutes before stolen by the dramatic entrance of an unannounced guest.

The book I was promoting was my seventh. In each, I had managed to include at least one or two celebrities of the past who seemed to have vanished since their limelight faded. To those whose lives are given over to seeing such people in person and getting their autographs, it is rarity that rules. My interview with Acquanetta, sometimes billed as the "Venezuelan Volcano" was a double coup. Not only had her whereabouts been unknown for many years, but in the interim she had also become the subject of a cult. Heterosexuals had discovered camp and her films, such as *Captive Wild Woman* ('43) and *Jungle Woman* ('44), were ridiculous even when they were current. In the former she played the title role, and yet had not a single line. In the late sixties a Manhattan theatre did brisk business with an Acquanetta festival.

It never occurred to me to invite her, because as the wife of a wealthy man, she traveled a great deal, often spontaneously, and she lived in Arizona.

The proceedings had been underway for about fifteen minutes. Orderly double lines had formed. Black mothers and grandmothers had brought their kids to see "Stymie". Queens were out in force to get a look at Ray Stricklyn, one of the pretty boys of the fifties. "Superman" enthusiasts were there for Kirk Alyn, the first to play the "Man of Steel" on the screen. The store's manager queued up patiently with his children. "Sheena" had her own following, mostly males, but with a smattering of female gym instructor types among them.

Much appreciated signatures were received and repaid by extravagant and most welcome compliments about "all the pleasure your movies have brought me over the years." It was an absolute love fest and then with a whisper from the promotion director, it got even better. A "Mrs. Ross" was parked in the waiting zone and wished a word with me.

It was Acquanetta sitting beside one of her grown sons who was at the wheel of a brand new 1978 Lincoln Jubilee coupe right out of the showroom their family owned. She was agreeable to coming in *if* I would escort her, present her and then get her right back to the car quickly. She only wanted to "Say 'Hello', give them a look," was how she described her plan to steal the show. It was outrageous of her and irresistible for me.

I had never before had so many people from my books in one place, and some were much sought-after by hardcore autograph collectors. I saw several I'd noticed on both coasts over the years, always hovered in doorways near celebrity haunts such as Sardi's, the Motion Picture Academy and the Beverly Hills Hotel. Spending a major part of their lives always searching intensely, hoping to spot a face/ "name" from the past, unrecognizable to most people, had developed in them a wild-eyed look. They, I knew, would go berserk when they saw Acquanetta. The atmosphere was reminiscent of that in the final scene of *The Day of the Locusts*.

Using the hand mike, I told all assembled of the surprise guest. She could only spare a moment, had to catch a plane, but wanted to greet her many fans. It was her first personal appearance in over twenty years. They were asked to welcome the "Universal Pictures star of the forties, the 'Venezuelan Volcano,' the one and only *Acquanetta*!"

Did they ever. As soon as they heard her name the leaders of the autograph clique, queens all, let out screeches.

"*Acquanetta*, for God's sake!" hollered one fan right into my ear.

Many, most of the others couldn't possible have known who she was, but was like the cry of "Fire", it was heard and heeded by all.

A fat guy I'd seen around for years put two fingers into his mouth and made with an ear-piercing whistle. As I led her across the floor before the others, she held one hand upright acknowledging the applause and shouting. Then the movie queens began chanting her name with the same beat as the Alka-Seltzer commercial, "Acquanetta! , "Acquanetta!" Many of the kids joined in, "Acquanetta!", "Acquanetta!"

She walked beside me, acknowledging her public. Acquanetta looked just like what she was, a rich woman of a certain age in stunning condition. She could have been the owner of the horse that had just won the Kentucky Derby. Ray Stricklyn, the only person on the panel who knew for sure who she was, was having a hard time clapping because he was laughing so hard.

And then just as quickly as she appeared, Acquanetta was gone.

"Dagwood" muttered over and over that he had never heard of her, didn't know who she was. "Stymie" didn't know either, but he was sure she was "colored." What they all were certain of was that they had been upstaged. Darla insisted I had engineered the star turn and thought it a hoot.

Both "Buckwheat" and "Stymie", perhaps together, came to the funeral home to pay their respects. The two had remained in touch over the years since they had been "Gang" members.

When I spoke with "Buckwheat" shortly after Darla was interred* just across Santa Monica Blvd. from the funeral home he said, "Such a sweet, lovely person." Then added, "She was that nice as a kid too."

Only ten months later, I said "Good-bye" to him at the Angelus Funeral Home. Propped alongside his casket was a poster of him at about age eight in a white top hat and tails. As I was unlocking my car outside, "Stymie" got out of his and donned his derby.

He had spoken with "Bill," as we called him, only the day before. "Buckwheat's" son, a parole officer, came out to greet him. That was in April, 1980.

In January of 1981, I was back at the Angelus for "Stymie's" funeral. His famous derby hat rested on the lower part of his casket.

Whenever I spoke of *Our Gang* to lecture audiences, I showed slides of them as children and as they looked during the years I knew them. I would close that segment of my presentation with what I was told and what

---

* Darla Hood's remains are in the Abbey of the Sanctuary of Light, Corridor G-4, number 7213 of the Hollywood Memorial Park Cemetery.

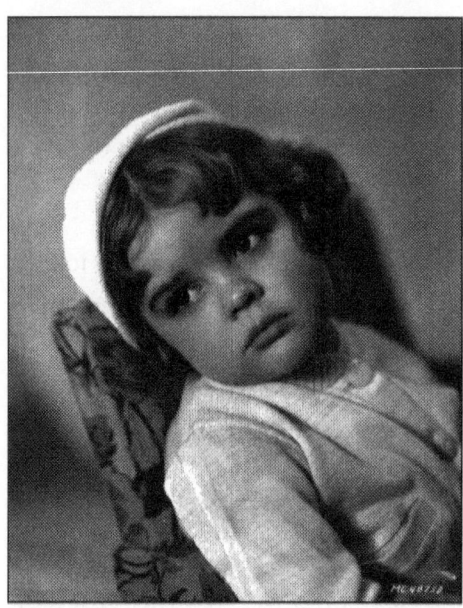
Darla Hood, "The Sweetheart of Our Gang."

I witnessed before I left Pierce Brothers Mortuary on the day I last saw my friend Darla.

I was seated, deep in reverie when I heard a couple enter the chapel from the rear. Even without turning around I knew from their voices that both people were on in years and that the woman was crying. "I don't want to see her," she almost wailed. "My little girl is gone. Looking at her body would just make it worse."

She all but collapsed in one of the last pews. The man walked to the front and up to her coffin. He acknowledged me as he passed, but we didn't speak until I was on my way out. Following me into the reception room, he thanked me for coming and asked if I knew Darla personally or professionally. The correct answer was "both," but I told him I had written about her and let it go at that.

"Because," he said, "She worked, or at least she worked at working, right to the end. In her carry-all bag she had with her when she keeled over were résumés and her most recent composites. Darla was a worker, she was."

From the chapel one could hear the sobs coming from the woman he had accompanied. I didn't need to be told she was Darla's mother. Nobody else could have cried out what she did after he had finally persuaded her to view the remains of her only child. I observed what transpired from the doorway. It was stated emphatically, without fear of contradiction. As to any guilt, we will never know.

Only a mother could have said, "Oh, Darla, you were such a very good girl and you had such a *hard* life."

One of the Little People

Just as there are people who throughout their lives mingle almost exclusively with the wealthy without ever acquiring much money, there are also those who over and over again find themselves in the company of famous people while remaining virtually unknown. These karmic magnetisms are inexplicable, even to those they affect. Neither effort nor intent appears to enter into such human chemistries. I have known a number of both types and found them lacking in any burning desire for or envy of riches or celebrity. This may be the very thing the monied and celebrated sense and are drawn to, those who don't want what they have. In their minds they are for once and at last being liked for themselves.

My comrade of many years, Jim Brennan, even before he moved to Hollywood from Canada at about the same time I arrived, was already well acquainted with quite a few luminaries although he was never in show business, nor did he seek to be. Jimmy, as he was known while in his twenties, was my age and had been raised in Windsor Ontario, literally walking distance from my hometown, Detroit. A tunnel and a bridge joined the two nations and many commuted frequently, even daily, between the cities. Brennan was still in high school when he began an intense affair with an adult, a personality known locally as a singer-emcee in shows on both sides of the Detroit River, which divided the two countries.

Although there was no perceptible difference in the speech or dress between Windsorites and Detroiters, crossing the border into Canada provided much greater freedom for Negroes, as African-Americans were then referred to, and teenagers because Canada was much less segregated than the United States and laws forbidding the sale of alcohol to minors, those under twenty-one years of age, were not nearly as strictly enforced as in Michigan.

Jim and I had seen each other around at various places in downtown Detroit before we met on Santa Monica's Will Rogers State Beach in 1953. By then, he and the lover he left behind had hung out together backstage at the Paradise Theatre, which was to the Motor city what the Apollo was to Harlem. At the Paradise, he had been introduced to such headliners as Dinah Washington, Billie Holiday and the comedienne Jackie "Moms" Mabley, as well as to the pleasures of marijuana.

On our first evening out together in Hollywood, Brennan and I went to hear "The Frantic" Frances Faye at The Interlude on the Sunset Strip. Afterward he brought me to her dressing room where I was presented to the raucous singer-pianist with Mercurochrome-colored hair. It was then and there I smoked my first joint, which was passed to me by Johnnie Ray. The "Prince of Wails" insisted I follow each toke with a sip from his thermos of Pernod over crushed ice, a delightful high.

Jim never said much about his background except that he was born out of wedlock. He revealed this to me early in our relationship, coloring the word "illegitimate" so strongly it was clear that even as an adult, the stigma was traumatic for him. He was raised in a small house behind a hostelry in downtown Windsor. A narrow alley separated his backyard from the loading dock at the rear of the hotel.

Because of family finances, movies were a rare treat for Brennan while growing up during the years of World War II, but he had access to a radio from the moment he returned home from school and listened intently while performing chores to help his working mother. One of his favorite programs *Captain Midnight* was heard over the local affiliate of the Mutual Broadcasting Company CKLW. That its studios were only a few blocks away made the strip show especially exciting for the pre-adolescent Jim. On one particular day in 1942 when the lady of the house returned from her job at the usual time and started making their supper, the serial was about to go on the air. Noticing that the trash from the day before had not yet been taken out, she pointed to it and said to her son, "Right *now*!" Just then the announcer cried, "Cappp-tainnn Midnight! Brought to you everyday…Monday through Friday…By the makers of O-Val-tine!"

Terrified that he might miss the opening of that day's segment, Jimmy threw open the kitchen door and leapt down the back steps. The instant he hit the ground he saw that the trash can was open. Rather than waste precious seconds in running to it, he lifted the big, greasy bag over his head, took aim as he had seen basketball players do in the gymnasium and sent it flying. The ten-year-old was strong, but no athlete. He overshot his target by several yards. The stained paper bundle cleared the alleyway and fell directly onto the aerial of the taxi being loaded. Brennan was sprinting back up onto his back porch as he heard an outraged adult voice call out, "Hey! What the Hell's goin' on here?!"

The back of the cab driver, who was bending over arranging luggage in the trunk of his vehicle, was littered. The bellboy opening the car's door for a departing guest was wearing eggshells and shredded cabbage, but the chief victim of the scattered garbage was the tall, uniformed man who was wearing, along with military decorations, potato peels and bacon rinds. He was staring at a major in the Canadian army, the brother of their country's future governor general, and Jim's first in-person star of stage and screen. The latter was, however, at that moment merely an actor without a script, because Raymond Massey was speechless.

Jim was living in Los Angeles for less than a month when someone took the starry-eyed twenty-year-old to a luau at the Bel Air home of producer Joe Pasternak. There, after opening a door that should have been locked, he came upon a very startled Dorothy Lamour-sitting on a toilet.

To my knowledge Jim never traded on his many contacts, and I doubt he would have had the nerve to ask for favors. He wasn't a malicious gossip or a name-dropper, which was probably perceived as discretion among higher-ups. Although he remained quite cute into his early thirties, he was not a heart-stopper, and he showed no professional ambition whatsoever. In other words, he would not have appeared as a threat to anyone. While such people seldom get anywhere in the sense of success as it is usually perceived, they go to a great many parties and have sex with a lot of people. What Brennan possessed was the quality of availability in that he would go to bed with anyone who attracted or impressed him and was willing to stay up and out to all hours and to take off for Palm Springs or Las Vegas on short notice, even in mid-week.

Throughout the fifties, Jim lived rent-free as the sort of housekeeper for a pair of songwriters. From time to time, he would work in some office long enough to qualify for unemployment compensation. These jobs were never with firms related to the entertainment industry so that he wouldn't encounter, and thereby embarrass, those with whom he slept or socialized. In the movie capital it is considered gauche to ask, "What do you do?" If your name is not recognizable and you don't volunteer your title, no one but an utter greenhorn will inquire. Unless you are a somebody in Hollywood, you are a nobody.

Weather permitting, Jim was to be found on the beach, getting the suntan that was derigueur among his sort. On cloudy days, he would breakfast leisurely at Schwab's Pharmacy on the southeast corner of Crescent Heights on Sunset Boulevard, a good place to make contacts and to be seen. If he didn't pick anyone up, he would grocery shop and then return home for what he called "housewifery."

By late afternoon, he would have meandered up to the 6300 block on the Strip to what had once been the salon of Hollywood's most famous couturier, Adrian. It was in our time the antique shop-office of James Pendleton, one of filmdom's ritziest interior decorators. Years before, the proprietor, acting in his position as the social director of Palm Beach's Roney Plaza Hotel, had charmed a semi-invalided heiress out of her wheelchair onto the dance floor. The end result of their awkward fox trot was a marriage lasting over forty years, which to even the most cynical wags appeared to be idyllic. Tall, handsome and always impeccably turned out, Pendleton's attentiveness and taste gave his wife the confidence to preside over the star-studded and "in" parties the couple gave in their Beverly Hills mansion.

If there was no client about or expected, the two Jimmys would gossip and giggle over what had and hadn't happened on the previous Thursday, which was Pendleton's traditional night out by himself.

Many of Brennan's late afternoons were often spent a few hundred yards west at Pupi's, a patisserie well known for its Raisin-Nut-Rum cake, which was served with heavy schlag. There one could linger indefinitely on its patio over an espresso or hot chocolate. He held court in a corner opposite Reggie Nalder whose deeply scarred visage was instantly and startlingly recognizable to fans of horror movies as well as those who had seen *The Man Who Knew Too Much* (1956) or *The Manchurian Candidate* (1962). The Austrian-born character actor's ghoulish appearance didn't inhibit him from cruising or from scoring. Jimmy laughingly explained the friendly competition between them by saying, "After all, it's not as though we're the same type. I'm an eight plus." Nalder's line about himself was, "I will *not* be treated as just another pretty face."

After I relocated to Manhattan in 1960, Brennan and I kept in touch sporadically, but in 1965 when my *Whatever Became of...?* show went on the air, he became a major source for guests. By then, he was employed full-time at Celebrity Service and had immediate access to telephone numbers and addresses of a great many of those I sought to interview.

I encountered quite a few famous people on both coasts and while on publicity tours for my books, as well as those I interviewed. Brennan met celebrities, and sometimes very unlikely ones, seemingly without effort or purpose.

While on one of the many trips I made to Los Angeles during the thirteen years I lived in Manhattan, I was entering the lobby of the swanky Sunset Tower just as one of the elevator doors opened and he stepped out along with two men I didn't recognize and one whose face was known throughout the entire world. John Wayne, like the others, was what my grandmother would have described as three sheets to the wind. The four men literally reeled from the building and out under its canopy to the limousine awaiting the star and two of his companions. Jim was left at the curb to fend for himself. Even if he had been sober enough to drive, he couldn't have because he had forgotten where he had parked.

"As glad as I was to run into you last night," he told me the following day over the phone, "You're the last person I'd want to see me with the Duke stinko. You'll be getting laughs out of that ridiculous scene for years to come, but thanks for the ride home. I've got such a fucking hangover and my car, by the way, was towed. Shit!"

It was an incongruous and funny sight, the macho movie star with an obvious queen and two "suits." One of them was a producer with whom Brennan had been drinking at Scandia's bar close by. "It just happened," was his explanation. Somehow he found himself tagging along to Wayne's suite where at their host's insistence, they all got stupefied drunk. Fortunately, a call from Mrs. Wayne prompted her husband and the other men to join her at Chasen's for dinner. That was Jim's chance to absent himself because John Wayne had begun to turn from quite surly to flat-out abusive. They never met again.

Although neither of us ever mentioned it, Brennan did not invite me to go along to any of the many dos he attended. I reasoned this was because I lacked the reverence he had toward those who had "made it." I enjoyed meeting acclaimed personalities, but I was not in awe of them. This would have made him apprehensive because studios, offices and residences are private turf, tantamount in Hollywood to a royal court. Good manners, as they are perceived anywhere else on earth, count for nothing. Adulation and ass-kissing are absolute musts for the "little people," which is what Brennan and I were considered.

By the time I moved back to the west coast in 1973, my career had taken off, but the unspoken something between us had become twofold.

Anyone else who hosted and produced his own radio program and authored a popular book series would have automatically have been on the "B" guest list. Because of the nature of my work, however, I was about as welcome as the Grim Reaper. Agents, personal managers and publicists visually recoiled at the mere mention of my name. Those who were not absolutely secure professionally as well as socially, which is to say almost everyone in the city, did not wish to be in the same room with me. I had become "that guy," the one who fielded questions on radio and TV shows about the whereabouts and activities of marquee names of yesteryear who were now considered "back numbers."

But the karmas of Jim Brennan and Richard Lamparski had blended perfectly because about the time I resettled in Los Angeles, he had taken a job with AFTRA in which he was in charge of members' files. This meant I could get from him the telephone number of anyone I sought to interview. Even if the person was inactive in his or her profession, they kept current with their union for insurance purposes and so they could be reached by casting directors. This was our secret because what he was doing for me was strictly against rules.

Jimmy was now Jim and although no longer what could be thought of as a party boy, he was still on the guest list of many of the hosts who used to invite him just to pretty-up a gathering. While his curly hair had thinned as his waist had thickened, he continued to be socially acceptable among his own kind because he always brought along a date, some young number others wanted to date. His reputation was for knowing a great many nines and tens who had not yet been passed around. Brennan could spot the type immediately and had a routine that seldom failed. His approach was, "How'd you like to go to the desert this coming weekend? You'll meet Liberace and God knows who else because his place is a Mecca for V.I.P.'s." The newer the face, the more unsophisticated they were, the more appealing the predators found them. His line to me about his technique was, "They get the message. I'll deliver if you'll put out."

I was invited to, but missed the one party Jim Brennan gave in his entire life. Returning from Europe to my Manhattan apartment in the autumn of 1972, I found a note requesting that I be one of the "few friends who put up with my behavior for *too* many years." It had taken place during the summer and was to celebrate the first anniversary of his sobriety. I don't believe he ever drank alcohol again, but whenever we were together, and often during telephone conversations, I was highly suspicious that he was high on another substance. I knew it wasn't grass because the one sharp exchange we ever had came about when I offered him a drag off a joint. "That's what the beaners smoke," was his haughty reaction, seemingly without recall of the many times he and I had used the substance together in the fifties. But he was now a member of Alcoholics Anonymous.

Like so many of those with whom I had spent my youth, Brennan deeply resented turning forty. Ignoring what we were being told from all sides, he continued to smoke cigarettes and eat red meat and sugary desserts. He was pushing fifty before he was forced to admit his addiction to some kind of pharmaceutical. I learned of his habit it 1984 when Jim called me from a locked facility where he had been committed for ninety days. I was asked to be the one visitor he was allowed that week and was admonished not to bring "anything" with me except a copy of the just published autobiography of one of his favorite screen actresses, Janet Leigh. My facetious reply, that I would sooner be caught with heroin and a set of works on my person than such rubbish as *There Really Was a Hollywood*, did not amuse the attendant who was monitoring our telephone exchange.

In 1986, Jim suffered a severe heart attack. After undergoing triple by-pass surgery, he recuperated in a nursing home. When I visited him there, he complained bitterly about the tasteless food served to him thrice daily. By way of celebration, I asked him to dine at a restaurant of his choice as soon as he felt up to going out.

It was on our way to dinner that night that I asked whether he ever went to the beach. Not for years, but one afternoon following the operation it occurred to him that fresh air and the sun could only speed his healing. One glance at himself shirtless in the mirror, however, and he realized he would have to go somewhere other than the one where he and I had spent so much of our youth. Young homosexuals do not care to look upon men with serious middle-age spread, much less a chest bearing deep, angry-looking scars around the heart area. Brennan drove instead a few miles south to the sandy shores of Venice, where he was much less likely to encounter anyone he knew.

It was a weekday and there were very few people about. For at least half an hour he prostrated himself, eyes closed, with his portable tuned to an easy listening station. This, he thought, had been a good idea because the ocean breeze and the warmth of the sun had put him into the mellowest mood he had experienced in quite a while. When the theme from

Ruby Gentry (1952) began playing, he sat up and folded his arms around his knees. Running through his mind were its lyrics: "They say, Ruby, you're like a dream. You're nothing like you seem."

There was a well put together, grey-haired male strolling along the shore, his feet making small splashes in the surf. He was a type Brennan had once heard me describe as a "magnificent ruin." This one had the gait and hauteur of an actor and there was something vaguely familiar about him.

Aware that he had been noticed, but without altering his leisurely pace, the man headed his way. This made his observer somewhat apprehensive because he had no interest whatever sexually in those his own age.

Without a word, the stranger sat on the sand alongside Jim's blanket, and after a moment began humming the dreamy "Ruby."

"Your line at this point," I interjected, "was, of course, 'Shall we dance?'"

"Don't heckle," he replied and continued telling of how they had sat together without a word between them for "the longest time." Rather than break the spell cast by that music, so familiar to anyone of their generation, he switched off the radio after its conclusion.

Jim felt the meeting was like the opening scene of a movie. "Yes, but a foreign movie," I suggested. Well, exactly because when the mature, handsome man did finally speak, it was with an accent, but more Latin than Continental. And once he started he didn't stop. Nor did he look at his audience of one. Instead, he stared at the ocean and told of how he and his wife had been living for many years abroad. He was from South America and she was German-born, although each had been to Hollywood sometime before, separately. This was long before they were married, or even knew each other. She had another husband in those days, a big English star. She was a star, too, but perhaps not so big. He had seen them together on Broadway in *Bell, Book and Candle* (1950) when he was a young man and developed a huge crush. So beautiful and soignée. It never left, the crush. He was still very much in love with his wife although things were not what they once were because she was "*too* sick." They had come back to Los Angeles because the form of cancer she had was very recently found to respond positively to a new treatment available only here. She was then in the hospital and would remain there for a few more days and then come back and they would be together until it was time to return. It, what the doctors did to her, left her very, very weakened and was very hurtful to her vanity. She was, after all an actress, which as they say is something more than a woman. Sometimes after she and he were together again, his wife would have this wonderful, almost rebirth and it would last for as long as two or three hours. Her mind would quicken and she would become very amusing, which was always her way until the disease struck. The divine Viennese accent that had so beguiled him in his youth would be hers again, no more slurred speech. This time was like a flash-back in a film because the color returned to her cheeks and her dark eyes would glow once more as she flirted with him.

At this point Jim's pardon was begged for telling him what he had. It was just that he found it so much easier to share these very personal matters with a stranger.

When his wife became, fleetingly, her old, or perhaps he should say "young," self, again, they would make love. It was sweet and passionate, but there was, of course, a desperation in it because each time might very well be the final one and both knew this.

It was during the afterglow following their last sex that she had said to him something that he had been savoring ever since. In that intimate, knowing, accented voice that had captured his heart years before, his wife had mused, 'We are so very lucky, you and I. We still feel this way about each other."

Following a long pause, his monologue delivered, the man stood and, brushing the sand from himself, thanked Brennan for his "kind attention" and hoped he hadn't upset him because he was feeling so much better for having expressed himself.

Jim, who never spoke a word throughout, asked whether I could figure out from what had been said who the man and woman were. Carlos Thompson, a sort of road company Fernando Lamas, hadn't made much of an impression on U.S. moviegoers opposite Lana Turner in The Flame and the Flesh (1954), but since then had become a successful film producer in Europe. Only a week or so before this, I had read of the death of his wife, Lilli Palmer.

Carlos Thompson's *Variety* obituary, four years later, stated that he had been severely depressed ever since and had committed suicide in his native Argentina.

Brennan had picked The Palm, a West Hollywood eatery with a saloon-like ambiance, complete with sawdust covered floors and cheeky waiters. It was known for generous portions of high quality, rich fare, hardly what someone on a very restricted diet such as he was assigned should have been eating.

"I hate salads," my guest snarled when I ordered one. It seemed his mother had often served them, insisting they were "good for me." What he wanted was the lobster bisque followed by a marbled steak with a side of cottage fried potatoes. That I passed on dessert didn't make up for the white wine I sipped throughout my starter or the frosted seidel of draught Beck's with which I washed down my entrée. He neither admired nor envied that I had no problem with alcohol and that I could resist the crème brulée without a struggle. He visibly seethed with rage over both.

Because he did not yet feel up to driving, I picked Brennan up and drove him home. It was on the return trip that I announced to my passenger that when the tenth volume of *Whatever Became of...?* was published, my publisher was going to take over the nitery in the Hollywood Roosevelt Hotel for a celebration to which I would invite one hundred of my favorite interviewees and a few friends. I knew of no one who would be more thrilled to be among so many of the myriad screen personalities he and I had spent our nickels and dimes to see when we were kids. By then, he would have fully recovered and would delight in being seen at such a function, especially now that he had shed over thirty pounds.

Brennan began then and there to speculate on whom he might bring. Just as I pulled up in front of his apartment building, the perfect choice came to him. The guy was ideal, he explained, because "Even *you'll* like him." For years we had a running joke over our opposite tastes in males. "We'll never quarrel over a man," a remark I made after being introduced to one of his dream dates almost thirty years before, said it all. My eyes glaze over at the mere sight of midnight cowboys and muscled, suntanned aspiring actors.

I turned off my ignition at Jim's insistence so he could tell me just why he thought I would want to meet this particular number. What he then related had never been revealed to anyone else before. It was not a story that would have gone over well in the movie capital because no one would have identified with either party. That is they wouldn't wish to see themselves in either role.

Even the guy's name was androgynous, the most appealing quality to me in both genders. Carol and Jim had first met in a department store elevator that was stopped between floors by a brief power outage. He was neither in nor of the entertainment industry. He knew the names Liberace and Paul Lynde, but politely declined a chance to meet either. He had never heard of Ross Hunter or his mate and fellow producer, Jacques Mapes, but after Jim offered to take Carol to the next brunch at Rock Hudson's house, phone numbers were exchanged.

The scene at "The Castle," as someone had named the star's large home at the top of Beverycrest Drive, had already been described to me by Stan Musgrove, assistant to the director Robert Wise and intimate of Mae West. According to him, about midway through his second Bloody Mary the man millions of women swooned and fantasized over became "minty." His humor ran the gamut from Carol Burnett skits to flatulence jokes. Among his inner circle, he was called by his original first name. "Most of Roy," Musgrove confided, "never made it out of Winnetka." He then hastened to add that the actor was neither cheap nor mean spirited. He believed, however, I would find him hopelessly square and corny. Brennan had told me sometime before that the only curiosity Hudson ever showed in his presence was as to what people liked to do in bed and how they were hung.

Jim didn't know how Carol was hung or about his sexual tastes because the young man did no more than to consent to accompany him. He studied architecture at USC and had no wish to break into movies. He didn't even go to many and, although he liked Rock Hudson well enough, he was more a Steve McQueen fan. He had never met a celebrity and reckoned "The Rock" would be the one he was certain his family back in Nebraska would know.

By the time he followed Jim's car up onto the top of one of the hills of Beverly and through the big open gates on that beautiful Sunday afternoon, most of the guests had arrived, and their host had made his usual appearance down the winding staircase. There were, as usual, only two types, both male, in attendance. The middle aged hangers-oners bullshitted and joked with and snubbed each other while leering at and cruising the young cute, handsome and pretty guys strutting their stuff in and around the swimming pool.

Through a fence or from a helicopter to a not too observant onlooker, the assemblage might appear very casual. Certainly the clothing was, and the abundant food was served in a manner a more sophisticated guest might well term "down home" style. They were, however, abiding by a code of behavior, and it applied to both the fresh-faced, clean-cut young hopefuls as well as the dirty old men of all ages. The law is unwritten, and seldom voiced, because everyone playing the never-ending game of Tinseltown knows and adheres to it at work and at play.

Put simply it is that the star rules always and in all ways. On a movie set or the photo gallery, he (or she) gets "the take." The star is protected from physical harm on location by a stuntman and is saved from fatigue during a filming by his double. He is shielded from scandal by his lawyers and his publicists. The camera operator, the wardrobe people and the lighting director seek to make him look his best, which, more often than not, means because of their efforts he appears younger than he is or appears to be in person. They all do their best because the feature or the series has usually been financed by the use of his name. They are being employed if not by the star, then indirectly because of him. This means that whoever he is, wherever he is, in your home or his own, the attention is always focused on him. It is, therefore, a given in a social situation and most especially in his own home, that Rock Hudson would be allowed what could be called the pick of the litter. When all the posing, pouting, projecting and flirting has ended, he usually got to bed whomever he wished. That Brennan had been the one who had brought the one the lord of the manor wanted meant he was sure to be asked back. Carol was not only the favored one on that day, he was obviously so. As soon as he spotted the flaxen-haired, soft-spoken, remarkably confident six-footer, all of the others faded from potential leading men to dress extras. This meant that the rest of those present could begin to make their moves. The star had found his Mister Right for that night.

There was, however, a problem, and Jim, whose instincts about such matters were quite keen, sensed it after Carol reacted with barely concealed bemusement to the big eye he was getting from the big guy.

Hudson donned an apron and chef's hat and took charge of the grill once the coals began to glow and the filets mignon were brought out. Carol's father was in the meat packing business, so the cuts of the steaks impressed him until it became clear that they were all to be cooked the way the host liked his best, crisp.

The situation became quite sticky as the enormous hot fudge sundaes and coffees were being finished. Apprised of his guest's major in college, Hudson suggested he take him on a tour of his home, which, according to routine, concluded in the master bedroom. Carol admired the scale, if not the furnishings, of the residence and the various views. But when his guide segued into his seducer, the younger man was not receptive. There was to be no clinch or steamy fade-out. Instead the star got a friendly but firm "thanks, but no thanks" response.

No, Brennan was not his lover, nor did he have a steady boyfriend. No, he wasn't straight and it wasn't a matter of a religious hang-up. Why then, if being a fit fifty-five didn't make him too old for Carol, what was the trouble?

"You're Rock Hudson" was the answer and although it was one he must have heard before, the actor pretended at first not to understand that there was a flip side to fame, something celebrities encounter frequently but seldom, if ever, speak of.

When the director Rod Amateau helmed one of Joan Crawford's TV appearances, she came on to him. He told me she feigned flattered amusement when he explained that he just couldn't. "It would be like going to bed with the Statue of Liberty or Betty Crocker, for God's sake," was his line. "I can't screw an institution."

Carol's answer, however, which was essentially the same, appealed neither to the star's ego nor humor. "Look, I leave all that stuff at the studio," he lied. "We're just two guys, so forget about who I am on the screen."

If he could he would, but the young man was unable to get past the public image, so carefully crafted and highly publicized over the years.

"Call me Roy. That's my real name and that's who I really am," argued the famed suitor.

"No, you're not, at least not to me," replied Carol. "You're Rock Hudson and I'm not Doris Day and I don't wanna be."

Doris Day!? Hudson protested that he didn't see what Doris Day had to do with it. But he must have. It was simply denial of the corner that longtime worldwide stardom had painted him into.

When Carol revealed all of this that evening to Jim over the telephone, he guessed he shouldn't have added what he did at that point, which was, "If we were in bed together I'd keep expecting Tony Randall to pop out from somewhere and make one of those zany remarks of his." Still, those words did the trick. The star saw it was a no-go and gave up.

As the guest made his exit down the many stairs, through the foyer and out to the courtyard, the place was being tidied up by Mark Miller, Hudson's major-domo. He and George Nader, his life companion, smiled and waved "Good-bye!" as Carol climbed into his car. Brennan figured that even if they perceived from the Rock's expression or mood that he had been rejected, they would have pretended they thought a quickie had been consummated.

In *Sunset Boulevard* (1950), Norma Desmond (Gloria Swanson) was touted by her director-turned butler (Erich von Stroheim) as the "greatest star of them all" and she proclaimed imperiously, "Nobody leaves a star!" But Joe Gillis (William Holden) walked out on her all the same.

After listening to the story, I opined that Carol's dialogue in that scene was sharper than that in most of Hudson's films. All Brennan could think of, however, was that because of the turn-down, he had never been asked again to "the Castle" and now, of course, poor Rock or Roy was dead.

So was Jim Brennan from a massive heart attack just a few days before my publisher's party at the Cinegrill, to which he had so looked forward.

The Worst Story I Know

"What is the absolute *worst* story you know?", asked the eighty-year old Ellis St. Joseph. What the scenarist had asked was more than a question. It was a request and a challenge, as well. For as long as we had known each other he had sought to learn awful things about people, perhaps so he could believe he wasn't the only person who thought of himself the way he thought of himself. His way of life was proclaimed on a sign taped to the door of the refrigerator in his Beverly Hills apartment, "Think *negative*!"

In a movie Ellis would be best played by the sinister character actor George Zucco. By 1990 I had known St. Joseph for over twenty years. When I told this to one of his contemporaries, he wanted to know why I knew him at all. He was, the man added, "filled with schadenfreude and envy." I couldn't argue on either point, but there was a reason I had kept in touch with him since we were introduced in New York in 1969. Ellis St. Joseph was often able to zero in on people and situations with uncanny perception and, if and when he chose, he could be a riveting raconteur.

My favorite Ellis St. Joseph story can only be truly appreciated by those who have had dealings with the executives of the Academy of Motion Picture Arts and Sciences. Anyone who has knows how very seriously they take their awards, which are symbols of the most successful promotion in world history and little more. Each year, for months before the Oscar ceremony, Academy members and their guests (one each) were admitted to the theatre in the Academy's offices, which were then on Wilshire Boulevard, merely by showing a membership card at the door. Features, cartoons, documentaries and short subjects were screened from the morning through the evening, seven days a week, ostensibly so that those voting could make their selections for the "Best" in each category. This was the theory and it was what members of "the industry," as they aptly called themselves, told each other and, just possibly, believed.

One afternoon St. Joseph had taken me to the showing of a film that had been nominated as the Best Foreign Language Picture of the previous year. Before taking a seat, he decided to make a quick trip to the men's room. The prostate cancer that was to take his life three years hence necessitated frequent urination. As he came down the aisle a minute or so later, the house lights were still on and I was gazing about the auditorium and smiling. Ellis wanted to know what was pleasing me so.

I suggested he give the audience a quick once-over before the picture started. He did, but couldn't see why. There were no movie starts present, nor any great beauties, if that's what he was supposed to see. Whom had he missed? The people in that half-filled house made me smile because once again I had proved myself right about the Academy Awards. Present were old ladies, many with their bridge partners or nurses, or housekeepers, the mothers and mothers-in-law of Academy members. Then there were homosexuals in pairs, the friends and lovers of studio employees and teenagers, children of same, who had brought their buddies or girl friends.

I was smiling because I like being proved right about just who attends those showings, non-members of the Academy. In the evenings, the attendees were more young people on dates, older people, those retired from positions at studios, and, again, lots of homosexuals, most of whom were merely movie buffs.

Ellis hadn't noticed what I pointed out, but he understood and agreed immediately with what I was saying. By and large, those in the motion picture business, whether they be executives, players, secretaries, editors, whatever, have little interest in "product," as it is usually referred to, beyond whatever production they are working on, and even then, their only concern is for their contribution. The last thing those who work on or in movies want to do on their off-hours is to view films. About the last place you'll hear conversation about movies is among those who "create" them. In the mid-fifties, I worked at the *Ice Capades* under a man who had once headed the Publicity Department of Paramount Pictures. He told me without a speck of irony that he and the majority of the press agents he worked with made it a practice not to see the pictures they were assigned to publicize. The thinking, he explained, was, "If you don't see the junk, it's much easier to write about it. Lying's hard."

Norman Lear, thought for years to be one of the great creative forces in television, routinely had his executive assistant fill out the forms sent him for Emmy nominations and voting, "anyway you wish."

St. Joseph, who had penned screenplays for such diverse features as *Joan of Paris* (1942), *Taras Bulba* (1962) and *The Christine Jorgensen Story* (1970), told me that when he was under contract to RKO Pictures, his confreres who belonged to the Academy automatically voted for anything that was produced by that studio. Oscars meant box-office, and the better RKO did financially, the more likely they would keep their jobs. Exceptions occurred when a good friend or someone whose work you genuinely admired was nominated.

My companion wanted to know, "How else do you suppose Lana Turner or Nick Adams, for God's sake, were up for Oscars? How else could Dorothy Malone win one? *The Greatest Show on Earth* is unwatchable, and yet it not only won for its writing, it copped the Best Picture Award of 1952!"

By no means was everyone in the business a member of the Academy. One had to apply for membership and be sponsored. Ellis hadn't bothered to do so until recent years. In due course, he received a letter giving him an appointment before the Academy's board of directors, at which time he was to be presented with his membership card.

As he put it, "It was a convenience and an economy. For a reasonable annual fee, I could see practically any film I wished free because there are screenings all year long, several nights a week, and it's almost never crowded. If the weather's good, I can walk there, because I don't care to drive after dark. Or I'd take the bus because I live right off Wilshire. Invariable, I run into someone I know and can bum a ride home if it's cold or rainy."

St. Joseph found the formality of the card's presentation faintly ridiculous, and was completely unprepared for a query from one of the board members. "We welcome you, Mr. St. Joseph, to the Academy, but looking over your many screen credits, we couldn't help but wonder why it took you so many years to apply for membership?"

The man who had written dialogue for such stars as Charles Boyer, John Wayne and Paul Henreid was without a script and blurted out, "Oh, I suppose it was just the snob in me."

As to the worst, the "absolute worst," I told Ellis of what had occurred in 1969 after John Payne and I had concluded recording a radio interview. As was so often the case, it was when the tape recorder had been turned off that my subject really opened up. Only a week or so before, he had attended Robert Taylor's funeral, just months after their mutual friend Dennis O'Keefe had died following a long struggle with what Payne called the "Big C." The three had been close since the early forties and remained so through Taylor's divorce from Barbara Stanwyck and subsequent marriage to Ursula Thiess. During those years, John Payne had wed and divorced Anne Shirley and Gloria DeHaven. O'Keefe's wife since 1940 had been Steffi Duna, the Hungarian actress best remembered for having in-

John Payne in the 1940s.

troduced Noël Coward's standard "Mad About the Boy" in the West End production of *Worlds and Music* (1932).

I couldn't understand why Payne would tell me what he did because it sullied my image of Robert Taylor, and I thought less of his so-called "old friend" for having revealed it. What he said was that after Dennis O'Keefe became very ill, he Payne, had urged Taylor to visit him, but the actor had begged off, maintaining it would depress him too much. Payne insisted that, despite his condition, their friend retained the same breezy, upbeat attitude they had always so enjoyed. "Can't do it," is all Taylor would say, and according to Payne, declined to call on or phone Dennis O'Keefe.

I didn't bring the matter up with O'Keefe's widow when I interviewed her because I knew she was still in touch with John Payne as well as Ursula Thiess. One day in 1990, years after the piece I wrote on Steffi Duna appeared in my ninth book, she beckoned to me as I was leaving the home of her next door neighbor, the writer Robert Windeler, insisting I come inside hers for a cup of tea. I perceived, as soon as I got close, that she was seriously ill. Payne had died the previous December. When she mentioned this and that she had attended a service for him in the company of Ursula Thiess, I repeated what the late actor had said. She was appalled and at first found what I had told her unbelievable. O'Keefe's widow was adamant that Robert Taylor was a frequent visitor to their home throughout her husband's illness and that they had kept in close touch by telephone whenever he was away from Los Angeles. "They remained dear friends until the day Dennis died," Steffi Duna insisted. She had often thought to herself how difficult it must have been for Taylor, because he, too, was suffering from the same disease and knew it all the while. Robert Taylor's death from cancer came less than a year after Dennis O'Keefe's.

"Buy why would Payne tell such an ugly lie?" I asked Steffi Duna. Deeply disturbed, she could only shake her head.

It is likely that when Ellis St. Joseph found himself at so advanced an age unemployable in the film industry that he developed an objective perspective. With it must have come the freedom to express himself about the ways of Hollywood.

After enthusiastically agreeing that my story had been the absolute worst he had ever heard, the screenwriter proceeded to worsen it. It hadn't occurred to me that he could actually answer my question as to John Payne's motivation, but then that was St. Joseph's specialty, divining why characters do what they do. His explanation made perfect sense, given the behavior patterns of many actors and the value system of the movie capital. He delivered his pronouncement with all the authority of one who had been around for many years. Having sat in on countless casting conferences, Ellis knew well how things worked in the studios. The first thing he pointed out was that both Dennis O'Keefe and John Payne were merely leading men, whereas Robert Taylor had been, for many years, a star.

"*All* actors, however their careers pan out, want to be stars," he contended. "It's the star who plays the central figure. It's the star whom audiences identify with, leave the theatre thinking about, fantasizing over. It would never occur to him that you would or could be able to check out the facts with Mrs. Dennis O'Keefe. How many people have even heard of Steffi Duna? Who but you, for God's sake, would be taking tea with her?"

As to why Payne told such a lie about someone he had palled around with for all those years, St. Joseph thought it was because he wanted the role of the true friend, the one who was loyal to the very end. Robert Taylor, on the other hand, would be seen as the heavy. Payne was the good guy, the one everyone would like and admire.

Ellis reminded me that even though Payne had been unmasked as a liar, a false friend and someone who was willing to besmirch a buddy, the revelation would not play negatively in the moral climate in which we lived. No truer words were ever spoken about Hollywood than when someone said it was a place in which there was no such thing as bad publicity.

His closing lines on the matter were, "Here you are telling this to me and you can be sure that I'll repeat it. It isn't a Dennis O'Keefe story or a Steffi Duna story or even a Robert Taylor story. Throughout his career the actor never made what could be called a 'John Payne picture.' Posthumously, however, he has succeeded in making himself the center of attention, because why else would we, or anyone for that matter, be talking about him? Make no mistake about it, this is truly a John Payne story."

The Queen of Sex

A day or two after attending Mae West's funeral in 1980, I was speaking over the telephone with my mother who lived in Detroit. When I told her of how she appeared in death years younger than when I had met her only twelve months before, she replied "Well, her looks won't help her where she is now." Although she never saw the star in movies or in person, or heard her on the air or read anything she had written, like most Roman Catholics of her generation, she believed her to be vulgar to the point of obscenity. Her ways were what lead into what was referred to as the "occasion of sin." All sins of the flesh were considered mortal sins, grave offenses against God's law, and to be punished by an eternity in Hell. I've often wondered what my mother and others like her would have felt had they known that Mae West's interment at Cypress Hills Cemetery in Brooklyn was blessed by a Roman Catholic Bishop and two priests.

I recalled when classes at St. Ambrose School reconvened after the holiday recess of 1939-40, my homeroom teacher, Sister Jean Claire, warned the second graders about her. She was a "disgrace" and all of our faith were to stay away from her films. We were admonished to remind our parents of this because there was a new Mae West feature coming soon to Detroit.

In our house she was usually referred to as "*That* Mae West." My older cousins and fellow Ambrosians said she had talked "dirty" on the air when guesting with America's favorite ventriloquist's dummy, "Charlie McCarthy" in December, 1937. That broadcast, like Orson Welles' radio dramatization of *War of the Worlds* a year later, seemed to have been listened to by everyone, but me.

NBC, the network that carried the show, banned the very mention of her name. Mae West was pilloried by our pastor from the pulpit at

Sunday mass. William Randolph Hearst, publisher of the newspaper all my family subscribed to, the *Detroit Times*, wrote editorials castigating her and her pictures.

My cousin Bobby and I used to peruse its Sunday entertainment section together to see which new pictures were playing in the first-run houses downtown. From the ads we learned who was in them. This is

Mae West.

how we determined what we wanted to see eventually when they came to one of the six theatres within walking distance of our homes. When we read that W. C. Fields, a screen personality we revered second only to Erich Von Stroheim, was Mae West's co-star in *My Little Chickadee* ('40), we were as one. The fires of Hell be damned, we *had* to see it.

I couldn't then have articulated the qualities about her that so struck and amused me, but by the time I left the Cinderella theatre after seeing the Fields-West western, I was an enthusiastic fan. When during World War II the Cinema* which had a policy of exhibiting foreign films and re-releases, showed a double bill of *She Done Him Wrong* ('33) and *Go West, Young Man* ('36), Bobby and I collected empty bottles that we cashed in for the deposits** until we had sufficient money for tickets and the streetcar fare. In doing this, we disobeyed the dictates of our religion and our parents because neither of us was allowed to go downtown.

My cousin pronounced them two of the best movies he had seen in his entire eleven years of life, and I couldn't, but agree. To paraphrase the star, herself, it seemed that, whenever we were "bad" it worked out good.

In the early fifties when I first came into the "gay life," as it was just beginning to be called by homosexuals, I learned that Mae West ranked as one of the living deities along with Judy Garland, Tallulah Bankhead, Bette Davis and Marlene Dietrich. There were others, but none with the following these personalities had. Curiously, there was not a single male counterpart.

When she brought her night club act to Ciro's on the Sunset Strip in 1954 the tiny Ice Capades' costumer, Billy Livingston, took me. He was the first person I ever knew who actually spent time with the star. Seeing Mae West in person was exciting, but somehow less entertaining than expected. I found the muscles on the men she had about her to be close to grotesque and no one in the show, including the star, showed a scintilla of spontaneity. Even more disconcerting, although the audience was obviously delighted to be seeing her live, I sensed most of us could have finished every one of her lines for her. By then, I had seen all her films, some several times, and read a few of her stage vehicles. I supposed and hoped she was making an unofficial farewell tour.

Stanley Musgrove, who was director Robert Wise's right hand man, was also Mae West's public relations spokesperson. His unofficial duty

---

* Since renamed The Gem.
** 2¢ on the regular size and 5¢ on the jumbo.

The Mae West beach house at 514 Palisades Road, Santa Monica. Courtesy of Paul Gilbert Adrian.

was to bring the star together with the kind of young men they both fancied, bodybuilders. The arrangement worked swimmingly for both of them because he became well known around town as the guy who could get you an introduction to the living legend. It was the perfect pick-up line for the type. Even big, slow-witted pieces of trade knew who she was and that she used weightlifters in her night club act and in her movies. It was also common knowledge on Muscle Beach that her beach house was lived in by guys she had grown tired of or were there on hold, so to speak, until "that certain party," her longtime companion Paul Novak was going to be away. Because Stanley had vetted them, meant they wouldn't "turn to dirt," the dread of all of those of a certain age who seek the sexual services of men many years their junior.

I don't know whether Miss West insisted that they be stupid, but most of those around Stanley, and he always had several living at his house, bordered on the moronic. The brightest, the only one I ever heard say more than a few words was Virgil, his main man. This one exception always impressed me as being very loyal, attentive, and protective of Musgrove who often needed looking after. Stanley was able to control his drinking, in that he was always cold sober when he was working. During his free time, however, his drunkenness ranged between the bleary-eyed to the falling-down state.

He was a longtime close friend of my colleague George Eells, biographer of Cole Porter, Anita O'Day and Ethel Merman, among others. Ironically, he drank hardly at all and Mae West not only abstained completely, she would not allow even slightly intoxicated people to be in her presence.

In 1977, shortly after George informed me strictly *entre nous* that he and Stanley were collaborating, but very much on the quietus, on her biography* I took him to a New Year's Eve party at the apartment of Lorenzo Tucker. Although he was known chiefly for his starring roles in all-black motion pictures of the pre-World War II years billed as the "Black Valentino," Mae West had him as leading man in her stage vehicle *The Constant Sinner* in 1931. In it she was a prostitute and he played her pimp. Eells, who believed Tucker to be deceased, was both astonished and delighted.

Like so many stars, Mae West did not like anyone to write anything about her that she hadn't first approved. That one of her inner circle, Musgrove, and a frequent guest in her home, George, both of whom she liked and trusted, would conspire to do such a thing would be seen by her as treachery and betrayal. That she would not benefit from their book financially would have infuriated her.

Over the years I came to know a number of people who saw Mae West more or less regularly at her apartment. The sixth floor of the Ravenswood on North Rossmore Avenue and/or at the large house she owned at 514 Palisades Beach Rd. right on the Pacific Ocean. Not one of them ever told me anything that made me especially want to meet her, and although they all quoted her over and over, she didn't seem to be coming up with any new dialogue.

The only Mae West line I ever heard that hasn't been repeated ad nauseam was told to me by Louise Brooks when she and I spoke a few hours after the world learned of her death in 1980.

When I remarked on her inventive use of the English language, comparing her with Gertrude Stein, Louise told me about being with her one night at The Abbey, a speakeasy owned by Miss West's close acquaintance, the gangster Owney Madden. There was another woman at the table, a non-professional who almost whispered at one point that she wanted to ask the star about "something personal."

As Louise explained to me, "For some reason our dates were elsewhere, in the boys' room or at the bar, because it was just the three of us at

---

* *Mae West*: A Biography by Eells and Musgrove was published in 1982.

the table. She was terribly impressed with us, a movie actress and a big Broadway star, and nervous about her question.

"Shoot," said Mae.

"Well, in your play, *Pleasure Man*, you have women, quite respectable ones, having relations with colored men. Sexual relations. You have them going up to Harlem just for that purpose. You even suggest some of these men are gigolos. I know you're going to laugh at me for being so naïve, but are there really such women? I mean, who seek out colored men?"

Mae West gave Louise one of her famous looks before she answered. It conveyed, "We know, don't we, honey?

"Mmm, there're a lotta types of that type," was the reply.

I especially liked that trademark "Mmm" sound she made to preface her more important utterances. It drew attention, sounding so post-coital.

I might never have met Mae West if I hadn't been at a loss as to how to entertain a sixteen-year-old girl who was staying with me over the Thanksgiving weekend, 1979.

The original idea was that she, her parents and her twenty-two month old baby son, who lived in San Francisco, were to be my guests. Zeena was her name and she was the daughter of Anton La Vey, the founder to the Church of Satan and author of *The Satanic Bible*, a close acquaintance of mine for over ten years.

Zeena's mother, who went by the name Diane La Vey, phoned to say something had come up to prevent her and Anton from coming. The grandparents were, however, willing to baby-sit their grandson Stanton, freeing Zeena to come by herself. Would that be all right?

The challenge I faced by consenting was that she didn't know anyone, could not drive, and wasn't interested in boys her age, not that I knew any. Her sexual appeal was a decidedly mixed blessing for me because with huge china-blue eyes and full pouty lips Zeena could have been sent out from Central Casting to portray the teenage daughter of the Black Pope. She could also have played the younger sister of "Little Annie Fanny," the cartoon character who appeared regularly in *Playboy* magazine, except her wardrobe looked like it had been chosen by pin-up queen Betty Page.

I would have felt much more confident in taking Zeena to Musgrove's had George Eells, who was the more sophisticated of the two as well as being sober, been present. To minimize the risk, I invited myself and my houseguest for drinks only, actually only one because she was underage and I was driving. I explained to Stanley that we were expected elsewhere for dinner and that my young friend absolutely longed to meet the "Queen of Sex."

Before George Eells learned that Stanley was having Mae West and some others in for the traditional turkey with all the trimmings on the holiday, he had agreed to go to a restaurant with Natalie Schafer with whom he was staying. When Musgrove asked him he had to decline since the star and the character actress had not jelled the one time the author brought the latter to a small gathering at the beach house.

Contrary to what many believed, Mae West did have a handful of women she considered friends, but they displayed the same deference toward her as did the men around her, and they were all what is politely referred to as "of a certain age."

Having a baby at the age of fourteen might strike a lot of people as precocious at the very least, but Zeena was woefully unknowing about the ways of aged sex symbols. I took great pains to impress upon her that the eighty-seven-year-old woman might very well be instantly threatened by a young girl, especially one who was built, as we used to say in Detroit, "like a brick shit house." Her miniskirt and spike heeled pumps could only exacerbate the impression.

By the time we arrived in Mission Hills, Zeena had worked herself up into a state of jitters. It was a case of adolescent shyness compounded by stage fright. Through her father she had been exposed to Jayne Mansfield, Barbara McNair and Sammy Davis, Jr., but they were merely stars. Mae West was *the* star as far as she was concerned. There wasn't anyone else in the entire world she would rather meet.

The only anxious moment I had came as I locked the door of my car and we started to cross the street from Stanley's house. Parked in the driveway of 11010 Arleta Avenue was a 1965 black Cadillac limousine. Before I had a chance to point out that it belonged to the guest of honor, Zeena blurted out, "Look, a hearse!"

Any allusion to death, aging or illness was absolutely, utterly forbidden in the presence of the woman she was about to meet.

Actually, nobody *met* Mae West. One was presented to her.

One look at Zeena and Stanley became extremely apprehensive about doing that very thing. It never occurred to him that my young companion might be female, much less a dirty old man's dream as well as the fantasy of most young guys. Fortunately, none of the other guests, all male, reacted strongly to her appearance. The two older queens present smiled approval of her outfit, but knew better than to make a fuss. The others, five or six weightlifters, were friendly enough, but seemed no more interested in her than they were in the four of my kind.

Despite the homeyness of the setting, crushed rayon velvet upholstery and shag carpeting all in autumnal colors, the atmosphere was court-like. Except that the chair, which resembled a throne, in which the guest of honor sat, was not in the center of the room, but off against the west wall facing into an alcove. I reckoned that this was so she could not be stared at and to assure that she would need to speak only to those persons permitted to come before her. Also like a court, I got the distinct impression that everyone knew his place and was being careful to keep it.

At my suggestion the host introduced me to Mae West and then disappeared into the kitchen. When I thanked her for the many times her work had brought me pleasure, I colored that last word, mindful that it was one of her favorites. I didn't allow Zeena to emerge from behind my left shoulder until I sensed the diva was comfortable with me. Then I told her that the young lady she was about to meet had come all the way from San Francisco just for the *pleasure* of making her acquaintance. This didn't leave Zeena much to say, but that was the idea.

Standing behind La West in the cloud of her Joy was a tall dark man with extremely broad shoulders wearing a midnight blue suit, matching tie and white shirt, the uniform of a chauffeur or a bodyguard. Paul Novak served both of those functions, as well as having been her live-in companion for twenty-six years.

All the time we were there, her main man stood, very erect, with his hands resting protectively on the back of her chair. George Eells once mentioned that one of Novak's duties was to carry with him a packed of publicity stills. Miss (she passed on the Ms.) West liked giving autographs or being asked or both, and he lit up when I whispered my request for a couple into his ear. While she signed the portraits, I finished my drink, thanked the host and said my "good-byes." Zeena awaited me at the door.

When Novak passed me an envelope containing the photographs, I stepped in front of Mae West again to tell her that my young friend and I had never felt more grateful than we did on that Thanksgiving Day for our shared experience and the pictures that we would treasure.

We had just reached the curb when Novak came down the front steps at a clip to tell us, "Miss West is pleased." "Pleased," the past tense of "Please," from the French root "plaisir," meaning pleasure. *Pleasure Man* was the title of the play she wrote and starred in on Broadway in 1928, and her novel published in 1975.

My guest and I had our dinner at Oscar's Wine Bar. Throughout Zeena talked about how lovely Mae West's skin was and of her tininess. When we returned home, I found a message on my answering machine. Louise Brooks wanted to hear how it went. I told her that La West had made with her famous "Mmm" grunt when my lips brushed the back of her tiny pink hand.

"That was very Paul Cavanaugh*" of you, Richard," she commented. "She must get her ass kissed all the time, but the hand is quite another matter. I'll bet that was the Polish in you asserting itself."

One year to the day later Mae West died.

George Eells had to get the OK from Paul Novak through Stanley for me to attend the services because they were private. When we arrived a little before two-thirty at the Old North Church of Forest Lawn in Glendale, it was shut tight.

A couple of dozen of the eventual over one hundred attendees milled about on that cloudy day. Most of them were of an age when just standing is an effort. My nature is to make, what are to me, amusing remarks in such a situation, but everyone else seemed serious to the point of grim. Obviously, they cared very much about the deceased, so much so that I didn't hear anyone grumble about being kept outside until almost fifteen minutes before the service.

Pecking order is always so obvious in Hollywood. No sooner had Rona Barrett, then the doyenne of filmdom gossip, alighted from her Rolls Royce than both doors swung open and we were welcomed to the strains of an organ medley of songs associated with Mae West.

Harry Weiss, Esq., whose standing among his colleagues within the legal profession was about on a par with what Roy Cohn's was in New York, stood out even in that almost all-male assemblage. His clothing was an only slightly subdued version of what he wore playing a Mafia don-like character in *Sextette* ('78), the deceased's last film.

---

* One of the great smoothies of stage and screen during the thirties and forties. He was leading man to Ruth Chatterton, Joan Crawford in their vehicles and to Mae West in *Goin' To Town* ('35).

Kevin Thomas, a feature writer-reviewer on the *Los Angeles Times*, was there. The journalist, a longtime member of Mae West's inner circle, sat in the same pew with another of the star's few women friends, Sybil Brand, the well known civic activist. Whatever she did, and she seemed constantly to be doing something, was always deemed noteworthy of prominent mention in the local press. Some thought this was due in major part to the fact that her husband, Harry Brand, headed the publicity department of Twentieth Century-Fox. The Los Angeles County women's jail was named for her.

Virgil pointed out Sam Gold, the founder of Gold's Gyms, to George and me. We both recognized the eight-time Oscar-winning costume designer Edith Head from her trademark dark glasses and bangs. Once again, I was to regret the smart-ass remark I had made about Judy Conova's lifestyle on radio a few years before. She took a seat across the aisle from us, but when I was pointed out to her, glared and then moved to the rear.

Producers and housemates Ross Hunter and Jacques Mapes were two of the other celebrities. Also present was the flamboyant, if quite frail-appearing, Criswell, whose "Criswell Predicts" newspaper feature was known nationally. The seer guested frequently on TV shows and was now and then the brunt of a joke by *The Tonight Show* host Johnny Carson. George Eells named him the "Prophet of Predictable Predictions," meaning he always told Mae West what she wanted to hear. I suspected that was pretty much the case with everyone around her.

While the mighty Wurlitzer throbbed out "After You've Gone", I spoke briefly with Bert Goodrich, who was comforting two very tearful young musclemen. My readers knew him as the first Mr. America, having won the title in 1939. When I interviewed him, he told me quite proudly, of his closeness to Mae West.

Suspense and surprise are so important in showmanship. Mae West, the self-invented world figure, was as successful as a showwoman as she was at sustaining stardom for over half a century. Her stock in trade was shock and her mourners were given a big one when Stanley Musgrove emerged from behind the velvet curtain that separated all of us from the casket. It was he who set the murmur racing throughout the chapel. Contrary to what we expected and what Paul Novak confirmed to the press, we were going to see her.

After her corpse was embalmed and dressed, he had brought in the cosmetician who had made her up before any public appearance. When the professional finished, Novak, after a long and close inspection, had given the ultimate accolade, "Miss West is pleased."

For years Mae West had suffered from severe diabetes. She had been hospitalized several times since I had met her. For a period of eleven days, she lingered close to death in the intensive care unit with Novak keeping vigil.

The reposed Mae West in the chapel's soft light could have passed for a very well preserved, healthy sixty year old. Furthermore, her expression was wonderfully peaceful. If it accurately reflected how she felt, wherever she was, her friends could take heart, because she looked to be serene and in a state of quiet pleasure. There was no trace of the snarl she had developed in recent years.

George and Stanley went up to view her together. Both thanked Paul, who stood at the head of the coffin as he had that Thanksgiving Day behind her chair, profusely for his decision to have it open. Musgrove was shaking and had to be helped out by Virgil. I was behind a quite expensively dressed old man, who walked as though he might be used to a cane. After a long look at the figure surrounded in satin, he almost yelped, "You're sure looking good, hon. May God rest your..." and then completely dissolved as Novak and one of the bodybuilders caught him. This while the organist segued into "Frankie and Johnny."

The one element I felt the scene lacked was the star's signature fragrance, Joy. The sprinkling of "The World's Costliest Perfume" around her remains would have been a nice touch, and one that would have pleased Miss West.

The mourner who most fascinated me never joined us, although she came to the cemetery. Mae's younger sibling, Beverly, sat out the service in her limousine at the curb. The sisters had the kind of intense love-hate, on-again, off-again relationship of well over eighty years that is found only between blood relatives.

When I first was in New York City for the summer of 1955, I had a caprice with a young public relations man who had been with the financier-presidential advisor Bernard Baruch during a lengthy lecture tour. He regularly accompanied Eleanor Roosevelt when she made personal appearances. When I asked him to tell me what they were like, he laughed and said he didn't know. He then described to me a state of being I found difficult to imagine and yet I couldn't not believe him. He said neither she, a septuagenarian nor he, an octogenarian, ever spoke to him unless they found it necessary. When they weren't in the privacy of their homes, limousines or an elevator, when no one could observe them, Mrs. F.D.R. and the elder statesman would remain perfectly still, usually with their eyes closed. When it came time to rise or walk or talk, they did so instantly. He insisted both were absolute professionals about doing whatever they agreed to do and were working on all cylinders then, but as soon as the engagement ended and there was no further need to make the effort, they retreated into what he felt was not a form of sleep, but a deep rest. "Conserving their forces," was his phrase.

What he described is what I experienced with Mae West on that Thanksgiving. Until I was right in front of her, she appeared completely lifeless. She reminded me of one of the waxen figures inside the glass of a fortune-telling machine, except their eyes always remain open. She sat motionless, her smooth hands resting on the arms of the chain, then, as though someone had dropped a coin in the slot, her long, carefully applied eyelashes lifted revealing the deep blue eyes that had looked so many men up and down with such thoroughness. It was like having the high beams of a marque trained on you. All of whatever my cousin Bobby and I were so drawn to years before was at once very evident. Call it star power or personality or "It." The quality was there still and in spades during those two brief exchanges.

Mae West's public image was of a completely independent woman who chose her men, then set the standards and rules for her relationships with them. I have never heard anyone who knew her suggest it was not so. According to both of her biographies* this, indeed, was precisely how she had lived her long life.

Whenever it was suggested that Mae West was really a female impersonator, she was incensed, although the star admitted she was a cinch for men in drag to impersonate. I believe the rumor lingered because there was never any indication that under all her artifice and attitude, she had a heart.

Mae West's popularity throughout the years with homosexuals of all ages and nationalities is well established and easily explained. Her outlook, tastes and values were the same as theirs with the insistence on hard, youthful bodies and gave none too subtle hints that size definitely *did* matter. She saw the male not as a life partner, but as a sex partner and a sex object.

---

* The second was *Becoming Mae West* ('97) by Emily Wortis Leider.

Older homosexuals especially identified with her attitude of sexual entitlement, the firm belief that money, fame and influence entitled her to intimacy with males young enough, in some cases, to be her grandsons.

Bette Davis once asked her if she had ever had sex with women. Miss West replied that she was "Too busy elsewhere," not that she was involved in a committed relationship. In other words, again the stance of the male, boasting of numbers, conquests.

As is often the case with world figures, Mae West was very complicated with more than a few seeming contradictions. Her pose was one of being worldly-wise, and yet she was unread, untravelled and unsophisticated. She was considered to be the "Most Quoted Woman in the World," but not one of her famous remarks could be considered "words to live by."

Perhaps the real paradox of Mae West was that her name was synonymous with sex, because although I've never known a guy who wasn't entertained by her, neither have I come across one who found her sexually appealing.

George Givot, the leading man in *Catherine Was Great*, her starring vehicle of the forties, told Eells of frequent invitations into her dressing room. He always declined because of her "mechanical" attitude toward sex.

Federico Fellini was quoted as finding Mae West "anti-sex," because he explained, "She always makes a joke of sex," which he found to be "anti-erotic."

Making a female laugh is often a major step in seducing her. It has the exact opposite effect on most males.

By and large one jokes about what he or she is uncomfortable with, things we feel guilty about. Those with eating disorders tee-hee about rich food, especially dessert. At Alcoholics Anonymous meetings the testimonials are peppered with references to "Martoonees," "A hair of the dog that bit you," "John Barleycorn" and as the world famous drunk and playwright Brenden Behan called it, "the gargle."

For all the males Mae West supposedly had sex with, not one claimed to have actually slept with her, including the man thirty-two years her junior whom she often described as "the greatest," Paul Novak. Her sister inherited almost all of her money. She rewarded his twenty-seven years of loyalty and servitude, which included the administering of the daily enemas, with a bequest of $10,000 out of an estate of millions.

A Rainy Afternoon in Beverly Hills

"Hey. You gotta stay at least until the downpour lets up. If you go now, you and Baby Dumpling'll get soaked." So spoke my comrade of many years, Fat Shelly. He was right and there was no real reason my St. Bernard and I needed to leave, anyway. We had stopped by his house on Betty Lane in Beverly Hills after doing some shopping, but she was perfectly content to lie in front of his fireplace, and I liked nothing better on a rainy afternoon than to schmooze and lift a few. His other guest, the slapstick comic Soupy Sales, was rolling a jumbo joint expertly. Good company, fine weed and a glass or two of Australian white. Let it rain.

Even the music was to my liking, an audio tape of jazz, featuring Soupy's son, a musician who was living with the daughter of the movie stars of the forties, John Payne and Gloria De Haven.

I had known Shelly Davis since the late fifties when he was producing the first in-your-face TV personality, Joe Pyne on Channel 5, where I was working. Even then, he was fat. During the sixties, he was in the nightclub business, his final venture being the wildly successful, original Whiskey a Go-Go on the Sunset Strip. By 1980, he was absolutely immense, resembling a Semitic version of the Latino comedian Porcel.

Whether or not there was any truth to the rumors about Davis's backing, I never knew, but I more than once heard him deny that he had any mob connections. "Just because I'm a big Jew from Chicago who ran joints on the Strip doesn't make me a gangster," was his response to any insinuation. But there was also a matter of his close friendship of many years with Allen Smiley, who was seated across from fellow mobster Benjamin "Bugsy" Siegel when the latter was shot to death.

I had no problem with Fat Shelly Davis' reputation, and he appeared to have none with my sexuality. "You're certainly fag-friendly, I once head someone say to him in a somewhat accusatory manner. His reply set everyone in the room straight, so to speak.

"Look," he replied. "I was a fat kid. I knew plenty of young queens in high school. Most of them were smart as Hell and some were very funny. They liked me, but I knew they didn't dig me, so I never went through what so many guys never get out of, if you know what I mean. Then I went to work in show business, which is almost as gay as it is Jewish. When I was running the Interlude and the Crescendo on Sunset, they were among my best customers. It was gay guys who put me onto Phyllis Diller before she happened. I played her for peanuts and she was a smash because they turned out in droves. They're very loyal to the old-timers like Sophie Tucker and Martha Raye. Queens are always the first in the house to get the jokes. They lead the applause and they drink like fish. So, what the Hell's not to like?"

Soupy had been a musician before turning to comedy. Off-camera he was crude, but never to my knowledge cruel. He played to the guys in the band and at the bar. That he used "fag" and "nig-nog" and "heeb" never bothered me. I had guested with him over NBC radio in New York where he didn't throw the pies he was famous for on TV. I found him on mike to be completely professional and frequently funny. In a social situation he employed my favorite form of humor, stories in which the teller was the brunt of the joke.

When I arrived, the two were talking about Anita O'Day, who had just opened locally. When I mentioned that my colleague George Eells was working with the jazz singer on a tell-all biography*, Fat Shelly made a face. I had not yet met her, but to me she had a flawless technique and a unique way with a song. Davis had no quarrel with her artistry. When she was booked into one of his rooms, O'Day did good business and behaved professionally. What still upset him, however, had taken place on the afternoon of her opening a few years before when she and her agent had come by his home to sign the contract. Shelly had excused himself to take a call from the east coast in his bedroom, leaving the two in the living room. His teenage sons from his first marriage were seated at the dining room table doing their homework.

The phone call took longer than he had anticipated. Anita O'Day evidently had become impatient because in his absence she had proceeded

---

* *High Times, Hard Times* (1981)

to shoot up heroin rather than wait until getting back to her hotel. Fat Shelly, who never did more than smoke grass or snort an occasional line of cocaine, was still angered over the incident. Either or both of his kids could easily have seen her fix right in their own house. So could have his wife, who minutes after the paraphernalia had been replaced in O'Day's bag, returned from the hairdresser.

A perfectly timed clap of thunder brought about a change of subject. Soupy wanted to know if I had ever met the second Mrs. Davis, whom he described as a "fine looking chick." I had not, and I could see from Shelly's expression that, conversationally, we had just gone from bad to worst. I had been told by mutual acquaintances that she was a looker who had run off with her psychiatrist. What I didn't know until that afternoon was what had disappeared with her.

By then, the man of the house had switched to Stolichnaya on the rocks. Passing me a somewhat bogarted reefer, he exhaled, at my suggestion, into Baby Dumpling's anxious face. My animal was pleased to receive marijuana in any form it was proffered. Our host then proceeded to confide in us the details of his wife's exit. As he put it, "She wasn't happy just to stick the knife in, she had to break it off."

"Sex and money," Fat Shelly often said. "What the fuck else is there?" Having walked out on her husband, his spouse was unlikely to have been awarded alimony. They had only been married a couple of years. The nitery business at that time was cash transactions. His two partners were from Las Vegas, where skimming was de rigueur. Although each of the couple had keys, his safety deposit box was in the name of Mrs. Davis, just in case the I.R.S. looked into his holdings. The amount of money his wife had taken with her was almost to the dollar what he had paid for the three-bedroom hillside home he had purchased a few months before their marriage. There was nary a thing he could do but cry, which for a moment I thought he was going to do into his icy vodka.

"The fuckin' you got for the fuckin' you'd gotten," was Sales' comment.

Now we really needed a *fraicheur* and Soupy, entertainer that he was, rose to the occasion. My dog's snoring was almost drowned out by the torrential rain. "Such a total hang-out calls for the story of my New Year's Eve, 1975-6, wouldn't you say, Shelly?"

The pudgy one scurried into the kitchen, returning with another bottle of wine and a large bowl of Beer nuts. "She was dynamite," he enthused. "A young version of Rita Hayworth, complete with widow's peak. Tell it all, Soupy. Don't hold back." Clearly, Davis had heard the story before, but he was amused at the prospect of a repeat performance. He had humiliated himself. Now it was Soupy's turn.

Every December 31st, Shelly invited a few friends for what he described as "a few drinks, some laughs and a good meal." His girth was mute testimony to the Lucallan feasts he prepared and his dos drew quite a varied crowd. The prominent internist Dr. Ray Weston and his wife mixed with the doyenne of celebrity gossip of that time, Rona Barrett and her husband. The actress Linda Christian, formerly Mrs. Tyrone Power, and the scenarist Ivan Moffat were regulars. Kitty Kelley made an occasional appearance as did Rodney Dangerfield and the former shoe king Harry Karl, the ex-spouse of Debbie Reynolds. The conversation could be about recent developments in medicine or current scandals or vivid recollections of a once prominent Hollywood figure. Vulgar language and ribald humor abounded.

Shelly Davis, a former holder of a liquor license, had only one rule and enforced it strictly. Nobody was permitted to drive home drunk. Another guest could take him home or he could stay in one of Shelly's guest rooms.

On the night Sales told us about, five years or so before, a well known personal manager brought as his date the heart-stopping redhead who was the central figure in his tale. When she was introduced to the comedian as Amber, her eyes told him clearly "Perhaps." By the time everyone sat down to dinner, her escort was stinko, and it was obvious she had no intention of leaving with the guy who brought her. "What a way to start off a new year!" was Soupy's thought. It soon became obvious to all present that she was warm for his form. As the entrees were placed before them, the auburn-haired beauty, seated across from him, had slipped off one of her shoes. While lifting the first forkful to his mouth he felt one of her warm, silk-stockinged feet nestle in his crotch.

Over coffee in the living room, Amber purred to Soupy that, traffic being what it was on that night, she wanted to leave elevenish at the latest. There was a little something she had to take care of at the Beverly Hills Hotel, which was on the way to his place; if he didn't mind.

After they had bid the others "Good-night and Happy New Year!" his score slipped into what she referred to as the "little girls' room" in the foyer. "No," she replied with faint amusement at his request. He could not watch. As soon as the door closed behind her, Soupy tapped on it and murmured, "Then how about if I get in the tub?"

They drove down Coldwater Canyon and pulled into the driveway of the pink palace. She wouldn't be long. The hotel's attendant permitted him to park in the circle where, as it turned out, Sales ushered in 1976 by himself. Frustrated as he was, he couldn't go looking for Amber because he had no idea which room or bungalow or suite she was in or what business she had there at midnight. By the time the lady of the evening re-entered his car he was beside himself, but as its door closed behind her, he got another waft of the White Shoulders she was wearing. It was then he received his first kiss of 1976 during which Amber sucked his tongue.

"I hope you had a little nap," was her entrance line. "Because you need to be well rested for what all we're gonna do later."

Instant absolution. But the "later" was not to be for a while. First she had to "look in" on a friend up in Benedict Canyon. It wouldn't take more than a few minutes. A house just off Cielo Drive. He could be mad at her, if he felt like it. Anger and passion are, well, they go good together, Amber mused. With that she leaned over and ran her hand over his inner right thigh before stroking what Sales referred to as "mister inbetween" while sticking her tongue in his ear and then whispering, "I won't be long and you'll be so glad you did this for me because when I get you home, well, I'm gonna do things to you there aren't even words for."

"Don't talk dirty or I'll come," pleaded Sales and off they went. The Evyan fragrance, he disclosed to us, was what his first "piece of ass," as he put it, was wearing on that memorable night so many years before. Orientation so often makes a lasting impression.

At Amber's direction, he came to a stop before a smallish luxury home near the foot of Bella Drive which leads to Valentino's Falcon Lair. There he waited and he waited amidst the cloud of cologne that lingered.

It was now gone two in the morning, and Soupy was more than hot and bothered. He was pissed-off. Here he was, less than a mile from where he had met this dame. It was dark and cold, and he had been parked in someone's driveway for almost an hour. Exasperated, he got out of the car and marched to the front door. He pushed the doorbell and heard soft chimes resounding within. No response, so he gave it another ring, followed by an impatient knock. Moments later, the door opened.

"It was at that point," he told us "that I knew I was in a 'B' picture and Amber, of course, had the lead. Her co-star was standing in front of me in a silk robe, complete with scarf. One hand is in his pocket and the other's holding, natch, a cigarette. Not only is this guy doing George Raft, he *is* George Raft, man. So, what would George Raft say to a complete stranger who's pounded on his door in the middle of the night? Just like he would in a fuckin' movie, George Raft says, 'Y-e-a-h?'"

Told he was looking for Amber, the man of the house informed him that she would be out presently. Right at the moment she was showering.

"So, what's my line in this scene?" asked Soupy. Without waiting for our prompting he continued. "What does, the chump, that's the part I was playing, the jerk who finally figures out he's been chauffeuring this hooker as she makes her late night house calls, what could he, me, say but 'Happy New Year! Mr. Raft.'? And he says back, just like in the movies, 'Right' and closes the fuckin' door."

But Amber with her red hair and White Shoulders, and of course the tongue, more than made it all worth while once they got to bed, according to Sales.

I believed Soupy and Davis expected me to reveal one of my misadventures of the boy-boy kind, but homosexuality does not, cannot, work like boy-girl relationships. Males and females can con each other over and over to a remarkable degree. For better or worse, homosexuals have each others numbers from the git-go.

My nature is not a competitive one. Which is not to say that aggression is not part of my make-up. My great endorphins come from doing things no one else has done or even thought of doing.

One afternoon a few months before that rainy one at Fat Shelly's, I guested on a radio show, on which I had been introduced as the "Man who's met everyone." I hadn't, of course, because most of the personalities I have encountered were entertainers, but in the host's mind, only show business people counted. The remark, however, must have gone straight to my ego.

That evening I dined with Billy Livingston, who for years designed costumes for Gypsy Rose Lee, Sonja Henie, Ice Capades and the Ringling Bros. and Barnum & Bailey Circus. He was a nattily dressed, perfectly proportioned, absolutely tiny man. Not quite a midget, but so small that all his shirts and suits had to be custom tailored and blocks had to be affixed to the pedals of his Cadillac. Billy was bi-coastal. In New York, he lived at the Hotel St. Moritz. When in Hollywood, he took an apartment in the swank Sunset Tower, the art deco home of celebrities such as Frank Sinatra, John Wayne and Doris Day.

After our meal, I drove Billy home and, at his request, accompanied him to the door of his suite, which I unlocked, opened and, after returning his key, said "Good-night." He was not a heavy drinker, but because of his size, his capacity for alcohol was very low, and we had been imbibing margaritas earlier in the evening and shared a bottle of wine with our dinner. Like women of a certain age, queens over fifty like to be seen home.

The concierge in the lobby was a magnificent ruin I had known since I first arrived in Hollywood in the early fifties. Then he was an aspiring actor and a knock-out. Our relationship was never close, but, for a few months circa 1956, it was quite intimate. As I approached the desk, he was just concluding an in-house call with: "The boy from Schwab's said there was no response when he knocked at your door. I figured you were napping. He left the prescription with me. I'll bring it up as soon as I can, but I'm all alone tonight because the doorman's home sick. You two must have the same terrible head cold. Yes, as soon as possible."

Turning to me, he said, "There's a candidate for one of your books. Zeppo Marx, the one no one remembers."

There were five Marx Brothers originally. The fifth, Gummo, left the team before they started making movies. Zeppo quit in 1934 to go into management. I longed to interview both, but neither of the letters I sent to the latter's Palm Springs home was ever answered.

I did not for an instant consider the right or wrong of what I did next. By then, I had acquired a strong sense of entitlement. I had met one of the five DeMarco Sisters, one of the two Barry Sisters, five of the Seven Little Foys, and two of the singing trios, The Pickens Sisters, the Boswell Sisters and the Andrews Sisters. Plus two of the three Ritz Brothers as well as two of the Three Stooges.

That I knew I would be intruding didn't bother me. The disingenuousness of my intended approach didn't matter. I was not about to be denied a single Marx Brother, a lesser one at that.

My chum behind the desk was delighted to allow me to take Marx's medicine to him. I could hear the hacking cough even before the door was opened by a rheumy-eyed, sixtyish man in a terry cloth robe. Taking

Duck Soup *(1933) was the final appearance of Zeppo Marx (second from the right) with his famous brothers.*

me for a bellhop, he wheezed, "Thanks," and then turned away to get "something for your trouble." I stepped inside, closing the door behind me. The man I was dealing with had only a severe cold. I was the one with a high fever.

Waiving away the gratuity, I launched into an extemporaneous spiel about how impressed I was to be meeting him and what an honor it would be if I could ask a few questions about his career. Career? What career? He hadn't made a picture in almost fifty years. Besides, he was "sick as a dog."

But surely he wasn't all alone. Was there no one there to look after him? Although it was not yet public knowledge, I knew perfectly well that his wife Barbara had left him for Frank Sinatra. Who, for instance, would make his breakfast? The Sunset Tower did not provide room service. Pointing to the kitchenette in his suite, he said, through sniffles, that all he needed was some coffee. He had a jar of Folgers Instant. He was going to take what Schwab's had sent over, get a good night's sleep and maybe he would feel well enough to drive home to the desert in the afternoon.

Marx was somewhat taken aback by my proposal, but he didn't say "no." I backed out into the hallway, wishing him a speedy recovery and stating that I would bring him breakfast elevenish. "We'll see," he mumbled and closed the door as a coughing spasm came on.

On my way out, I explained to the concierge that Mr. Marx wished neither calls nor visitors until I returned the following morning. We were to breakfast together. He was to leave a note for the person on duty at that time.

"Mr. Marx is expecting me," I said as I breezed by the desk. "Please let him know that his breakfast is on it's way up."

"*You*" is all my victim uttered when I stepped off the elevator. "I'm not hungry. I feel rotten."

"Starve a fever. Feed a cold," I responded while he stepped aside allowing me to enter.

"Hot tea, not coffee, with lots of lemon and honey. Not merely vitamin C capsules, *Power* C, Mr. Marx, bagels, still warm with orange marmalade. Eat. Eat," I said as I laid out the provisions on the coffee table.

I was told that I didn't look like a Jewish mother, but I certainly was acting like one. "What's this all about, anyway?"

It was about *him*, Zeppo Marx. He would nosh and feel better for it. Somewhat grudgingly, he admitted that the tea was nice and hot and the marmalade was delicious. Did I live in the building? How did I keep the tea so hot, then? The orange juice wasn't Tropicana. Tasted like fresh-squeezed? Who the Hell was I and what did I want from him? *Interview*? He hated interviews. Always had. Hadn't done them, hadn't had to since he quit the act, which he had never enjoyed being part of to begin with. It was his mother who insisted he be in it. He had always felt like a fifth wheel. Yes, he would like another cup and the strawberry jam looked good. He would try that on the second bagel. All he usually had in the morning was coffee, but this certainly hit the spot and he had to admit, it was nice of me to bring it to him. How much did he owe me? More goddamn questions?! Marx hated being questioned, especially about the past. What was that in my hand? It looked like a *camera*. He certainly didn't want to be photographed, looking like "something the cat dragged in."

"Don't take any," he pleaded just as the strobe light went off. For Chrissake, his bathrobe was partly open. As soon as he pulled it closed and tugged on its belt, I took another. "Enough!" he cried, but with the second flash I had gotten my cover shot.

As I packed up my thermos and empty insulated container, Marx grumbled and spit into wadded Kleenex. He was going back to bed, so I would have to excuse him. I was thanked, sort of. He hoped I had gotten everything I wanted although he had no idea what anyone would do with a picture of him in a bath robe, for God's sake. Gummo? His brother? He lived next door to him in the Springs. No, he certainly would not give me his phone number because Gummo hated being reminded of the years he had been on stage. He was retired and wanted to be left alone.

My host was in his doorway. I was standing by the elevator bank and had pushed the "down" button. "Say, this is the second time you've been here and I still don't even know your full name or what this was all about. Never mind. It's over, thank God."

I replied that he had started off the day the right way, with a hot breakfast and had made another person, me, happy.

"*You*, happy?! What the Hell do I care about making *you* happy? I don't even know you and, say, did anyone ever tell you that you're one very pushy guy?" He was going to try to forget the whole goddamn experience.

"Be that as it may, I've been made happy and *you*, Mr. Marx, are responsible and for that I'm very grateful."

His "Ah, shit!" resounded up and down the thickly carpeted hallway of the Sunset Tower as the elevator arrived and the door to Zeppo Marx's apartment slammed shut.

"You oughta be ashamed!" Fat Shelly cried, "Taking advantage of that poor guy and while he was sick and all." I had revealed a side of myself, a very unbecoming one, that in all the years we had known each other, he had never seen before. What he wanted to know was in which book of mine was the profile, so he and Sales could see the photo. There it was in the fifth series, an ailing, disgruntled old Jew in his bathrobe. He supposed I had sent Marx a copy, just to rub it in. And I had told the story with such glee. Where was my sense of guilt? Obviously, I had no conscience.

Soupy had made no comment. At some point during its telling, he had tumbled onto his side and was pounding the pillow on the couch. "Too fuckin' much," was all he could get out.

The rain had ceased and it was time for Baby Dumpling's dinner. As she and I started to leave, Sales had a thought. Hey, there was something Shelly had forgotten. When Zeppo Marx quit as an entertainer, he had become an agent for Chrissake. Agents didn't have the same rights as regular human beings because, well, they're *agents*!

"I'd forgotten he was an agent," said our host. "Soupy's right, of course. You get to do *anything* to a fuckin' agent. They all have it coming to them. Fuck Zeppo Marx! That was a great story."

As Baby Dumpling and I descended the stairs of Chez Shelly, my farewell was the same as George Raft's, "*Right.*"

LASSIE'S MASTER

I first met Tommy Rettig when I spent Christmas Eve, 1972, with him and his family on their Daisy Hill Farm near Arroyo Grande. Tom, as he much preferred being called, and his wife Darlene were raising their two sons on the outskirts of the small town of California's central coast. Their fifty-acre spread could have served as a location for the *Lassie* TV series that had made and kept his name and face famous throughout North America for years. After the cast he headed was replaced by another in 1957, the actor found he had a serious problem in that he seemed hopelessly typecast as the clean-cut country boy, Jeff, master of the legendary collie. This image, however, changed overnight and forever a few months before when he was arrested for growing marijuana on his property.

The law enforcement agents who conducted the raid made a thorough search and seizure of the premises, leaving the couple with not so much as a seed of the illegal cannabis.

"Darlene! Come see what Santa brought! Merry Christmas! Merry Christmas!" cried the man of the house as he struck a kitchen match to light one of the jumbo joints I had produced from my flight bag.

After that exceptionally mellow interview, which was followed by a delicious holiday meal (there were home grown walnuts in the turkey's stuffing), Tom Rettig and I were to remain in close touch until he died in 1996 at the age of fifty-four.

I knew him through his bankruptcy, the loss of his ranch to creditors and the divorce from the woman he had married when they were both seventeen. For approximately a year, he was almost totally blind. After a complicated operation restored his vision to normal, he mastered computer technology, and authored two books of software.

Tommy Rettig and the author at a book signing in 1978. The female at the actor's right is Lauren Chapin of Father Knows Best *fame.*

Twice he was arrested on felony charges. Because Tom knew I wished him well, but had no interest in hard drugs, we didn't talk much about either case. Neither resulted in a conviction.

Maybe if Tom Rettig had grown taller than five feet, five inches he would have been less recognizable, but even with a beard, fans often spotted him. Perhaps because his was a face they had seen on their home TV screens, rather than in a theatre, people who grew up watching Jeff Miller with his collie Lassie, walked right up to him and spoke very much as they would have to a playmate from years ago. The actor part of Tom welcomed these encounters just so long as he could extricate himself after a minute or two from a slobbering and often presumptuous admirer.

We had known each other for years before he explained my uniqueness in his life. I was the only person he knew who hadn't ever seen him on stage or screen. Not only had I never watched even one segment of *Lassie*, because of my aversion to Marilyn Monroe, I always avoided *River of No Return* ('54).

I don't know of any other child performer of his generation who had struck such a strong cord of identity with young viewers as Tom had in *Lassie*. Males fantasized about him as their older brothers or best friends. He as the first big crush for many girls, and not a few boys.

In the early eighties a stage producer I had known for years asked me to bring him and Rettig together. His plan was to star the actor in an off-Broadway musical in which Tom was to portray the artist Toulouse-Lautrec.

Until I introduced them, I had considered the New Yorker rather jaded about celebrities, but he appeared to be almost overwhelmed by meeting the hero of his childhood.

One of the questions I asked those I interviewed for the *Whatever Became of...?* books was which of their contemporaries they most enjoyed working with. Tom Rettig was far and away the most popular boy actor among boy actors.

"You're *This is Your Lifing* me again," he would say whenever I arranged unexpected reunions with those who had especially liked guesting with him on *Lassie*.

The even shorter Tim Hovey's opening line to Tom after not seeing him in many years was "*You* didn't grow any either."

When Tom Nolan, the star of TV's *Buckskin* series, declined, with obvious disapproval, a drag on the first joint of the evening we were to spend together, I passed it to Rettig. "Great!" enthused Tom. "That leaves all the more for us."

The biggest surprise I arranged for him, as well as the most successful, was having Billy Gray in the room between Tom's and mine at the Campton Place Hotel on Union Square when four of us were flown up to guest on the TV show *AM San Francisco*. The other was Marc Copage, whose TV exposure came after theirs playing Diahann Carroll's son on *Julia*. He was at least ten years their junior. "What sage advice have veterans Tommy Rettig and Billy Gray for this fine young actor at this point in his career?" asked our KGO-TV hostess.

"Save your money!" was their heartfelt response in unison. Everyone laughed, but Marc.

As far as I know Tom never got seriously involved with any of the many women he dated after the Rettig marriage broke up. Every one of those I met was considerable younger than he, but because of Tom's youthful appearance and manner, this was never obvious. I thought he summed up his attitude toward all of the females he dated when one evening in Musso & Frank's after he and I slid into our booth. He had just introduced me to the young woman he had brought who was making a telephone call before joining us.

"Dig it," said her escort. "She's going steady with Tommy Rettig, her mom's favorite."

Tom's parents separated shortly after their only child joined the road company of *Annie Get Your Gun* in 1946. When his father died in 1985, he admitted to me that they hardly knew each other. The evening he returned from the memorial service on the east coast we met for dinner at Oscar's Wine Bar across from the Chateau Marmont.

After we raised our glasses to the late Mr. Rettig, his son said, "I found out his morning that I'm not anti-Semitic. Until I met the other side of my family I never knew I was half Jewish. Whey couldn't I have been told this years ago? I'd have had more of a sense of identity."

Like many stars, Tom's eyes were quite large, almost goggled. He then turned them away from me, gazing at nothing in particular and asked ever so innocently, "Wonder what my line would have been if he'd turned out to have been Mexican?"

The boy he had once been was always very apparent in Tom Rettig. It was almost as though the fates, having withheld a normal childhood, had then rewarded him with an eternal boyishness. But that was how he came on, and everyone I knew who knew him responded to this quality. It is rare, especially in a straight male, and very endearing.

Within him, however, there ticked a different clock.

Suspecting the birthday he had coming up on December 11, 1981 might be heavy for him, I arranged a small do, Thai stick, Korbel's driest, Natural, and various things in puff pastry served hot before a crackling fire. After the others left, I asked the guest of honor how he felt about turning forty.

My friend smiled wistfully and revealed a side of him I experienced only this once saying, "I've been a professional since I was five years old. Not that acting and all the travel and learning to look after yourself is such a bad way to grow up, but it puts years on you. I'm a lot older than forty."

I thought of this remark immediately when Ron Alexander phoned from his desk at *The New York Times* in January, 1990, to read me what had just come over the wire: "Lassie star Tommy Rettig, dead of heart failure at 52*"

The tale he had to tell was, well, one he probably shouldn't be telling at all. He couldn't imagine anyone else revealing what he had experienced the day before, especially to a writer. A Hollywood writer at that.

---

* Born December 10, 1941, he was 51 years old.

He wasn't going to share it with anyone else, and neither could I. Not ever. I had to promise. It was worthy of Nathanael West. On second thought, it was even more Richard Lamparski's style. Because he knew how I got off on irony and humiliation. It sounded like the kind of story he and I had hooted and hollered over in the past. Of course, those times we were laughing about things that had happened to other people.

What he related took place during the three or four months he worked as a shipping clerk for a film distributor while he was free on bail.

Tom told it all, complete with gestures and expressions, when he was good and ready. He wasn't good and ready until after he got good and high.

He was free to leave work at 5:30 each day, providing all shipments had left the premises. The day before, an order had been phoned in a bit past five o'clock. The client was told that it would be about an hour before it could be prepared for pick-up. It wasn't yet six o'clock when a motorcycle roared up the alley and stopped at the shipping and receiving room's back door. He didn't get much of a look at the messenger who was taking off his helmet as he entered, but Tom felt he caught a glimmer of recognition. Anxious to finish up and head for home, he spoke over his shoulder, suggesting the man help himself to the coffee next to the postage meter and have a seat. There was to be about a five-minute wait.

The motorcyclist sat on a tall stool. For a few minutes, the only sound in the room was made by the typewriting of an invoice and then an address label.

The question that broke the silence had the tone of an accusation: "You're Tommy Rettig, aren't you?"

He thought his reply in the affirmative sounded more like an admission.

After a brief pause, the voice behind Tom said, "Well, I'm Rusty Hamer."

What did Lassie's master and Danny Thomas's TV son have to say to each other?

"Hi", was all either of them could muster. "Whataya' doin' these days?" was unnecessary and "How ya' doin'?" was out of the question.

Again there was a quiet in the room as Tom busied himself, tying cord around the cans of film and then taping them together.

What he heard next was "S-H-I-T!"

"He made it into three syllables," said my guest.

There was even more steam behind the even louder "F-U-C-K!" which came next.

Tommy and Lassie.

This was followed a minute later by the thump made when a boot collided with the trash can. Passing Hamer the package, Tom held the door open for him and said, "Well, we met at last."

"Yea. Wasn't it fucking great?" was the response.

My guest had helped himself to the Kleenex on my desk. "Of course, it would have been so much funnier if it had only happened to someone else," mused Rettig while wiping the tears of laughter that had begun streaming down his face.

January 1990 Santa Barbara: I never listened to phone messages or even glanced at the mail until I've had my breakfast, and made my toilet, and feel like it.

I didn't learn of Rusty Hamer's suicide until it was announced on KUSC's noon newscast. Somehow I had known he was working on an oil rig in the Gulf of Mexico. He was living in a small coastal town in Louisiana, which is where he was when he shot himself in the head with a .357 magnum.

Tom Rettig was about to sit down to spend another day at his computer when he learned of his contemporary's death over a morning TV show. When I returned his call, a CD of *Music For Airports* was playing and his ankles were resting on the banister of his balcony in Marina del Rey. While sipping a beer, he was gazing off onto the lagoon that flowed alongside his condo.

I told him that if I had my own TV show, he and I would fly with my crew to the funeral where Tom Rettig would tell about the time he and Rusty Hamer met.

I was quite taken aback by his reply. Although I couldn't see his expression and the line was delivered with a laugh, I felt he, too, was surprised at what he said: "In lieu of that, you are hereby given my permission to tell about it at *my* service."

The remains of both actors were cremated and their ashes were scattered at sea.

A Star Is Born

The most attractive man I have ever known, and there isn't even a close runner-up, possessed moviestar looks and the perfect name for a marquee, but a major part of his appeal for me was that he wasn't acting anything. Even when he appeared on two episodes of the TV series *M*A*S*H**, Clete Roberts was cast as what he was, a foreign correspondent. He could certainly have essayed the role of a daredevil pilot, because he not only looked the part, he was also an aviator.

Clete Roberts, along with being extraordinarily handsome, had a commanding voice, a large, warm personality and dash enough for several screen idols. Nobody, but nobody, looked better in a trench coat or spoke with more on-the-spot reportorial authority. Each of the many times I viewed his telecasts from various trouble spots around the world, he struck me as the kind of journalist who would be great fun to hang out with, who had stories galore, but who wouldn't spoil it all by getting drunk.

By the time I encountered Roberts, he was over seventy, but still active in his profession and in full possession of the élan he had always projected from the television screen. The timing could hardly have been better, because had our paths crossed before they did, I wouldn't have had anything much to say to him. A few weeks before then, however, I had heard him on a TV talk show mention a few facts about his background. We met a few moments after I pulled my car into a self-service petrol station on North Vine Street on a gloomy afternoon in late 1981 and proceeded to uncap the gas tank. At the next pump was Clete Roberts, every bit as tall as I had imagined and beaming his "on-the-air" smile. My immediate assessment was that he liked being recognized and enjoyed being who he was.

As the fuel began flowing, I introduced myself, adding, "If you have twenty minutes or so, I'd like to buy you a cup of coffee over which you'll hear a story you can tell your kids and theirs. In fact, they'll repeat it to their grandchildren, because it's about someone who was once a member of your family."

Off we went in separate cars to a nearby luncheonette where Roberts glanced through a copy of my most recent book. Having thus apprised himself of the work I had been doing for over fifteen years, the newsman sat back in the turquoise vinyl banquette, expecting, I believe that I was about to reveal something about his cousin, the prominent screen actress of silent pictures, Marguerite De La Motte, who had been Douglas Fairbanks, Sr.'s,

John Bowers was leading man during the period of silent films to Mary Pickford, Leatrice Joy, Corinne Griffith, Dorothy Mackail and Lillian Gish.

Marguerite De La Motte was leading lady to Douglas Fairbanks, Sr. in three of his silent swashbucklers.

leading lady in the silent swashbucklers *The Mask of Zorro* (1920), *The Three Musketeers* (1921), and *The Iron Mask* (1929). During the TV interview, he had said, in passing, that after graduating from school in the early thirties, he had come to Hollywood, where he was for a while her houseguest. He told, laughingly, of driving her big, luxurious Marmon convertible up and down Hollywood Boulevard. Although he didn't say so, the implication was that in the back of his mind was the thought that, just maybe, he would be "discovered." Clete Roberts in his early twenties behind the wheel of one of America's great marques certainly would not have gone unnoticed.

What I had to relate, however, was about his relative's husband, John Bowers, who had played opposite Mary Pickford in *The Eternal Grind* (1916). After being top-billed in at least half a dozen features into the mid-twenties and co-starring with Marguerite De La Motte in *Lorna Doone* (1923), he was leading man to Leatrice Joy, Corinne Griffith, Dorothy Mackaill and Lillian Gish. By the advent of talkies, however, Bowers had begun to "slip."

Because he and De La Motte had separated by the time the young Roberts arrived in the film capital, he never met the actor and knew nothing of the circumstances of his death. I related what I had been told by the scenarist Robert E. Carson, who shared an Academy Award for the original story and writing of *A Star is Born* (1937) with its director, William Wellman. The latter, had been a friend of Norman Kerry and had known John Gilbert, two stars of the twenties whose careers had gone into decline after talkies came in. Carson confirmed what I had heard for years, that the character of Norman Maine had been based on John Gilbert, whose heavy drinking brought about his death at the age of forty-one in January, 1936 and Kerry, who was well known within his profession for his outrageous behavior. Their contemporary, Lois Wilson, told me that she had once been speaking with Norman Kerry in the lobby of the Hotel Ambassador when a matrons' small dog nipped his ankle. Kerry immediately snatched the animal up from the floor and bit its rear end.

The writer conceived the character's surname when the producer David O. Selznick popped his head into Carson's office one day and asked what progress he had made on the script. Assured that the writing was going apace. D.O.S. then inquired as to the name of the star Fredric March was to play and was told, "Norman…Norman Maine." During the pause, the writer had glanced out of the window onto the sign "Maine Hotel," painted on the side of the building at the corner of Washington and Ince Boulevards, a few blocks from the studio.

It was the story that broke in November, 1936, that inspired the famous suicide scene in the first two versions of *A Star is Born*, where Norman Maine walks fully clothed at night into the breakers of the Pacific Ocean. By then, Marguerite De La Motte's estranged husband was working sporadically and only in quickies. Bowers was staying with his sister and brother-in-law almost directly across the street from where Clete Roberts and I had met. Before we left for the coffee shop, I pointed out that apartment house because it would figure in my tale, and told him that Man Ray, the famed Dadaist-Surrealist photographer, had lived there throughout World War II.

When John Bowers learned that his old friend Henry Hathaway was directing Gary Cooper and George Raft in *Souls at Sea* (1937) on and off the shore of Santa Catalina, the actor rented a sixteen-foot sloop and sailed to the island, hoping to land a part in the picture, only to learn that it already had been cast. The actor's sister, upon learning that her brother had drowned, admitted that he had been despondent over his career and had actually spoken several times of "sailing off into the sunset." The body of the onetime star, who was considered to be "all washed up" in films, had just washed up in the Santa Monica surf.

Clete Roberts had already viewed the star commemorating Marguerite De La Motte, on the Walk of Fame at 6902 Hollywood Boulevard, but followed me in his car up North Vine Street to 1709 where John Bowers had his, only a few blocks from his last address at number 1459.

Like any good journalist, he listened intently and took notes throughout our talk because, as he told me before we parted, "I'll be dining out on this one until the day I die." And, he also sought the story behind the story. How had I come to know Robert E. Carson and what was he like?

Carson, who also wrote the screenplays for *Beau Geste* (1939), *Western Union* (1941) and *The Tuttles of Tahiti* (1942), was married to Mary Jane Irving, a child actress in silent pictures. We had met one morning in 1975 when I interviewed her in their residence for my sixth *Whatever Became of...?* book. Ten years before, he had caused a stir at the memorial service for David O. Selznick when he explained the producer's fabled energy by dubbing him "Hollywood's original speed freak." It was the first time anyone had spoken publicly of D.O.S.'s addiction to amphetamines and the Selznick family took umbrage.

Had I been asked to speak at the funeral of Robert E. Carson, I would have repeated what his wife related to me about his reaction to the famous Bel Air Fire. On that fateful day, the sixth of November, 1961, the Carsons were shopping at Saks Fifth Avenue in Beverly Hills. When they stepped out onto Wilshire Boulevard the sky was black with smoke and pedestrians were abuzz with the news of how flames had so quickly swept down from the hills of West Los Angeles. The couple's big white colonial home at 10565 Fontenell Way was directly in the pathway of the advancing inferno. What, she asked anxiously were they going to do? Without a word he led her to their car and proceeded to drive eastward, away from the threatened area. They drove out of Beverly Hills, through the Miracle Mile, and were approaching tony Hancock Park when the distraught wife could contain herself no longer. "Bob, *Wherever* are we going?" was her question.

"Well, we can't very well go home and I'm hungry," he replied.

But they had passed the Beverly-Wilshire, the Brown Derby, as well as at least a dozen other restaurants. Mary Jane Carson's mind was on something other than food.

Their destination, he announced in his perfectly calm and very suave manner, was Perino's, the ultimate in continental dining in Los Angeles at the time.

Perino's!? Their beautiful home might be burning to the ground and they were off to Perino's. "*Why?*"

"Because, the fire might be stopped before it gets to our place," he replied. "In that event a celebration was clearly called for."

"And if it *isn't?*"

"Well," replied the screenwriter. "Then, you and I will be in the need of a really good lunch."

"That," said a beaming Clete Roberts, "is just what William Powell would say to Myrna Loy in a fade-out."

It was certainly a hard line to top or follow, but to my mind Mrs. Robert E. Carson came close in what she confided after her husband left the room to make a telephone call. "You see, Richard," she said, "that's Bob's attitude toward just everything, which is why after all these years I'm still in love with him."

Seconds later, when Carson returned, his wife told him what she had just revealed to me, adding that their residence suffered only minor smoke damage, but the home behind theirs had burned to the ground. Remembering what had, as well as what hadn't, happened always gave the lady of the house the chills.

"Well, it gives me an appetite" said her husband. "I hope Mr. Lamparski will join us for lunch. I've just made a reservation."

And off we went. Where else, but to Perino's?

A True Hollywood Romance

One afternoon in 1985 as KGO's Jim Eason finished reading a commercial, the show's engineer held up a forefinger indicating that there was exactly one minute before the hourly newscast would begin, thus concluding my guest stint over Northern California's most powerful radio station. My host, who was once described in a San Francisco newspaper as "The Jackie Searle* of the Air," challenged me in the time we had left to "Give us the bottom line on Hollywood," a city people write entire books about. He was asking me to be clever, but had I become flummoxed and embarrassed myself, that would have been, to Eason, equally entertaining.

I reminded the audience once more that I was to appear on KGO-TV's morning show the following day and that I would be signing copies of the latest edition of my *Whatever Became of...?* books that afternoon at a local bookstore. Then I did what he had asked, I stated my opinion of Hollywood, that it was probably the "most *unromantic* place on earth."

The tale I have to tell is, therefore, a most unusual one, because not only did it take place in Hollywood, but it is also of a male couple. I have known homosexuals who have seen their most extravagant sexual fantasies and/or professional ambitions come to fruition. Infinitely more rare, however, is having the dream of romance come true.

Although I didn't start interviewing celebrities of the past over the air until March 1965 I had had the idea since the late fifties while living in Los Angeles. By the last months of 1959, I had approached a number of personalities who were willing to see me, but I had what is called in radio "mike fright." That is, I was fearful I would freeze up once I came face-to-

---

* Jackie Searle, the child actor of the thirties, specialized in playing obnoxious brats. He is probably best remembered for his roles opposite John Barrymore in *Topaze* ('33) and "Cousin Sid" in *Adventures of Tom Sawyer* ('31). His unofficial title among screen buffs was "The Face You'd Love to Slap."

face with such a personality as Upton Sinclair, "King of the Muckrakers," or Amelita Galli-Curci, a diva of opera's Golden Age, or Vicki Baum, author of *Grand Hotel*, a smash hit as a book, a play and a movie during the thirties.

The once scandalous Evelyn Nesbit, known to my parents' generation as the "Girl in the Red Velvet Swing," was the ice-breaker because she insisted that we meet first for a friendly, informal chat before she would consent to be recorded. It went very well, but then we didn't have a recorder between us. What I needed was to conduct an interview with someone who, if I bungled, wouldn't matter all that much. By the age of twenty-seven, I knew that failure was one of life's best teachers.

During the Christmas holidays, I had tea with my comrade Michael Monroe, who, at approximately thirty, was still trying to get a career going as a young leading man. In ideal lighting on a good day, he could pass for twenty-five, but his type, the raffineur-lounge lizard, had gone out of fashion in movie making. He managed, however, to drive a late model Cadillac previously owned by Mrs. Eddie Cantor, dress well and live at the Villa Madrid. One encountered a great many young, extraordinarily good-looking people with that kind of mystique in Hollywood.

Michael's building was above Sunset Boulevard on Miller Drive. The apartment directly across from his was occupied by one of the screen's most prominent sex kittens, Terry Moore. His had once been the home of Tom Drake, about whom Judy Garland sang "The Boy Next Door" in *Meet Me in St. Louis* ('44). No sooner had I taken a seat than he told me that above us in the penthouse Glynis Johns and Robert Preston were "living in sin." One of our bonds was an appreciation for the expressions, life styles and personalities of the past. It was Michael Monroe, who, when I revealed my need, thought at once of the perfect solution. It just so happened that the subject he had in mind, Richard Cromwell, lived one door away at 1359 Miller Drive. I would certainly have a hard time to think of anyone else I would have been more nervous meeting, because he was my first conscious crush. I vividly remembered when my mother took me grocery shopping as a youngster, lingering under the marquees of the Lakewood and Cinderella theatres near our home on Detroit's eastside to gaze at the beautiful young man in stills from his pictures. I had always liked that he and I had the same first name.

"Funny you should call today of all days," he said when I phoned him as a follow-up to my letter. The date was January 8, 1960, his fiftieth birthday. He wondered, "Whatever will we talk about? I haven't made a movie in a dozen years." By then he had reverted to his original profession. When Cromwell was "discovered" for the title role of *Tol'able David* ('30), he was an artist. After he could no longer get roles in films, he had worked almost exclusively in ceramic tiles, which he sold through interior decorators. The bar of the recently opened Hilton Hotel in Beverly Hills had an entire wall of his work, and Burt Lancaster had commissioned him to create a mural of textured tiles for the dining room of his Bel Air home.

Richard Cromwell, circa 1935.

During his heyday, Cromwell designed and built his residence at 1359 Miller Drive. It had been so admired within the movie colony that he had a near duplicate constructed next to it which was now being lived in by his "dearest friend" Claire du Brey, an actress whose screen career spanned from silent pictures to *A Song to Remember* ('45). As my host showed me through his house, he remarked, I sensed very proudly, that Cole Porter had rented it from him for three consecutive summers during World War II.

His hair was a rather flat brown, but he had it all, and the eyes seemed every bit as large and as almond-shaped as they had on the screen. They were, however, bloodshot and bleary.

Richard Cromwell appeared almost embarrassed by his career and had nothing of any consequence to say about the stars he worked with such as Clara Bow, Gary Cooper and Bette Davis. Although he was featured in *Poppy* ('36), he and its star, W.C. Fields, had no scenes together and had never met. He had sculpted Greta Garbo and made life masks of two of the theatre's biggest stars, Bea Lillie and Katharine Cornell, but would or could not tell me anything about them. The only thing he volunteered about his career was that he was thankful for the money he made from acting because it had allowed him to provide well for his mother who had been left a widow when Richard, the second of her five children, was nine years old. His attitude to whatever I asked seemed to be, "But why would anyone be interested in *that*?" My final question, "What in your life has given you the most satisfaction?" sent him into the most prolonged of his many pauses. The answer appeared to surprise him as much as me: "Well, I guess it's that I finally was able to stop drinking."

The tape we recorded was unbroadcastable. The experience with my one-time heartthrob, however, was invaluable because I was never again nervous about meeting with anyone.

As I was leaving, Cromwell thanked me for my interest in him, allowing that he doubted anyone else would be. As fascinated as I was by this near-ghost of a screen idol, by then, I shared his relief that our time together was over.

He mentioned while showing me out that dinner guests were expected and when the front door was opened there were two coming up the stairs only a few yards away. Our host couldn't very well not introduce us. Martin Kosleck, who was in the lead, would have been instantly recognizable to any moviegoer of the thirties and forties for his screen portrayals of foreign spies, double agents, resistance fighters and Nazi officers, but he was known mostly for having played Hitler's propaganda minister Dr. Joseph Goebbels four times. One step behind was a blond male in his early thirties, not the same type as Richard Cromwell, but every bit as appealing as he had once been.

On October 5, 1960, my birthday, I moved to New York City. A week later, many of the missing pieces of the Richard Cromwell puzzle came together when I read his obituary. The vagueness and broken speech must have been caused by medication for the cancer, which had plagued him for sometime. The great irony was he had been recently signed to appear in a motion picture at Twentieth-Century Fox, his first role since 1948. The part was taken by Neil Hamilton, who had been a leading man when Cromwell was at his peak.

Ten years and three books later, I was on one of my frequent trips to Hollywood to interview personalities for my radio program and the next volume of *Whatever Became of...?* and had been invited to a private screening. I was taken by screenwriter-film historian De Witt Bodeen to a large home on the shore of Toluca Lake. Its owner, I was informed, was the attorney for the Harold Lloyd estate and an avid movie buff. Somehow he had managed to secure a print of a motion picture believed to no longer exist. When Warner Brothers bought the rights to remake *The Letter* ('40), with Bette Davis, it was thought that all copies of the original 1929 version had been destroyed.

The tension in the beautifully appointed screening room was palpable. De Witt was anxious to see whether the performance of Jeanne Eagels held up. He was in college when she had stunned him in the role of the Somerset Maugham anti-heroine. I had never seen the legendary star in any of her silents or her other talkie, *Jealousy* ('29)*, also thought to be "lost". Everyone present, perhaps a dozen, on that Sunday afternoon was on tenterhooks about the condition of the 35mm print, which was over forty years old and nitrate. When the remarkably clear credits came on the screen, there was a burst of applause stemming from relief of our apprehension. The sound was equally well preserved, and while I cannot say I preferred Eagels's performance to Davis's, there was no question that the latter borrowed from the former.

For me the feature's most interesting scene, and the only discernable difference between the two versions, comes when Jeanne Eagels makes the purchase of the letter she needs so desperately. After accepting the agreed upon money, the Chinese wife of the man she has murdered deliberately lets the envelope drop to the floor, forcing the Caucasian woman to bow before the Asian. The sensation of being there and seeing what we did was every bit as exciting, to me, as an opening night on Broadway. The atmosphere when the feature concluded was one of shared ebullience.

When Bodeen and I stood to leave, he spotted and waved to a male couple who had come in after we were seated and bade me to come with him to "Say 'Sieg Heil!'" to Martin Kosleck." The same guy was with him, and this time I got his name, Christopher Drake. It sounded actorish, but he was not a bit. Neither appeared to remember meeting me previously, and I didn't remind them then. Both, however, knew my name instantly.

They "adored" my books. Was I allergic to cats by any chance because they had seven and knew to warn people coming to their home for the first time. How about for drinks before I returned to Manhattan? "Vunderful, vunderful," said Kosleck as his companion wrote down their

---

* *Jealousy* was remade as *Deception* ('46), again with Bette Davis in the lead.

address and telephone number.

On my first visit I was with Bodeen, who soon after moved to Spain. I went by myself frequently after that and, following my return to Hollywood in 1973, sometimes included Martin and Chris at the dos I had in my home.

When in 1982 I assembled nineteen personalities from my books to inscribe, a la the Chinese Theatre forecourt, their names in the new cement pathway leading to my front porch, Kosleck was among them.

By then, his arthritis had worsened to the extent that Chris had to assist him in kneeling and then to his feet. Even writing his name with a chopstick in the wet cement was a real struggle because he had lost the use of three fingers on his right hand. Both men appeared delighted with the article I did on Martin in my seventh book in which there was no mention of their relationship. "So very discreet of you, Dritcherd," commented the actor. "Ve appreciated it, but ve really don't give a shit who knows." This attitude certainly set Martin apart from other homosexuals I called on for inclusion in my books. Michael Whalen and Tom Beck of the thirties, Lon McCallister of the forties and Ray Stricklyn of the fifties were among the many who sought assurances that I would not be making any references in their profiles to a "housemate" or "companion." Like Noël Coward, they did not wish to disillusion their fans. They may have lost their hair and/or looks, but their "image" must not alter.

Until the nineties, that sort of thinking was perfectly understandable to me and everyone I knew. I had, however, been sharply aware of its irony ever since an incident that occurred shortly after my first interview.

At a drinks party in the Lux Sunset Tower apartment of the costume designer Billy Livingston, I held forth about my hour or so in the company of Richard Cromwell until I sensed it was not being well received. My host, who was about twenty years my senior and a real enthusiast of my concept for *Whatever Became of...?*, confirmed my apercu after his other guests, four or five males of varying ages, departed. The younger guys were not a bit interested in what one termed a "back number" and their elders were ill-at-ease with the subject.

Billy, a tiny, dapper Texan, made me understand that I was being both naïve and gauche carrying on like that about Cromwell. "Darlin' don't you know that queens do not wish to know from men of the past? It dates them. It's only the old dames, no matter how decrepit they've become, that interest us."

After the profile I wrote of Martin was published he began to really open up about himself and some of the luminaries he had known. I had stated in print that he had been married to the titled German actress Eleanora von Mendelssohn, great-granddaughter of Felix Mendelssohn but made no mention of the fact that she had taken her own life. Perhaps in gratitude he told me that both of them had made several attempts at suicide. Shortly before he and Chris met Kosleck, he had jumped from the balcony of their fourth floor apartment which accounted for his deep limp.

Theirs was one of those unions impossible for even the parties involved to explain. I told Kosleck I could identify because I had such a relationship when I was in my early twenties with the star of silents and early talkies, Aileen Pringle, and conducted another, different, but every bit as intense years later, with Louise Brooks. No male has ever held the magnetism for me that both women had. It was equally charged on their parts, and yet we were never sexual.

"Ve vere vonce," chimed Martin. "Then Eleanora was simply my closest friend. Ve vere inseparable. She and I vere touring in Elisabeth Bergner's company of *The Two Mrs. Carrolls*. Ve vould lie on our separate beds in our double rooms traveling across America, telling each other about our disillusionments for hour after hour. She used to vow to leave all her money to a home for the brokenhearted. Vun closing night management gave a party and ve drank too much champagne. Or maybe it vas just enough champagne because it happened. Zo, vile she thought about whomever she vas thinking about, I vas doing likewise. But, Dritcherd, I hope I haven't shocked you vit my story of pre-marital sex."

Kosleck's condition was such that he could no longer do much more than supervise the care of the flowering plants that seemed to flourish all over their West Hollywood property. One afternoon as I came by for tea, Chris entered from the rear bearing a dish of floating gardenias he had just cut. Immediately, he and Martin began talking about their friend Richard Cromwell, who had said many times that when the time came for him to die, he would like to be smothered by a pillow filled with gardenias. It was then I spoke of the way he had been on that day we had first met fifteen years before. When I repeated what he had said about having stopped drinking, Chris told me that Cromwell's doctor, after disclosing that his cancer was terminal, suggested that alcohol might help in masking the severe pain he experienced during the last year of his life, but that he adamantly refused. He was determined not to "make my exit as a drunk."

"Gin vas his drink," interjected Kosleck. "Mine too, then. Ve used to say 'Lux for that schoolgirl complexion, but gin for zat schoolboy erection.'"

I knew that Cromwell had been briefly married to Angela Lansbury during World War II, but not that they had been introduced by Martin who had known her since she was a nineteen-year-old clerk in the cosmetics department of the very bon ton Bullocks Wilshire. After telling this to me, he added that when Cromwell was near death she had phoned him after a silence between them of almost twenty years. "It vas very dear of her, Dritcherd, because it made him feel so much better to know she vasn't embittered toward him or about their marriage."

Once when I was in their neighborhood I stopped by because I had Baby Dumpling in the rear of my Jeep and Martin had asked to see her. Both he and Chris came out to the curb to do so because their home and yard was the domain of all those cats. "How absolutely beautiful!" exclaimed the actor. "Like from F.A.O. Schwartz."

"We love dogs, too," added Chris.

"Yes," agreed Martin as a little boy and girl passed us on the sidewalk. "It's *them* ve despise." It had something to do with the picking of flowers from their fenced front yard and "all of the God damned noise they make." He was giving them his best Dr. Goebbels glare.

Zeena La Vey, Anton La Vey's youngest daughter, had recently relocated to Hollywood along with her boy, Stanton, who was my godson. Shortly after their arrival, I took him as a treat for his ninth birthday to view a white tiger. As only pre-adolescent boys can be into things, he was into all felines. They had brought both of his cats with them from San Francisco.

By then, I though I had known Kosleck and Drake long enough and well enough to raise their consciousness as regards to kids. I prepared Stanton by running *The Mad Doctor* ('41) for him. In it Martin played the very jealous companion of Basil Rathbone. All I said to them was that I was bringing with me my houseguest and that he was a cat enthusiast.

After being introduced, Stanton sat by himself quietly at the far end of the living room where he made immediate eye contact with the big Persian male perched on a stool in the dining room. Within minutes, it was on his lap. "Vatch zis vun take umbrage," predicted Martin of a dominative white female named "Queen Bea," entering from the kitchen. But

*Christopher Drake and Martin Kosleck in 1960.
Courtesy of the John Cocchi Collection.*

Stanton was well aware of the ways of both genders and managed to give each of the seven equal time and attention.

Chris brought Stanton a soft drink and a big pot of tea for the grown ups. Like Martin, he was impressed by the mutual attraction between the boy and their pets.

A plate of the thin, buttery shortbread Chris had baked hours before was passed around. Martin poured our tea. My godson sipped his cola.

I drew the boy into the conversation by mentioning that one of the local sights I had shown him and his mother was the facade and forecourt of Falcon Lair and that he was more impressed that its present resident was Doris Duke rather than Valentino the original owner. "Vy?" Martin asked. Simple. She was the richest woman in the world, *and* she was still alive. "Good thinking!" complimented our host and then suggested his companion take their young visitor for a tour of their home and backyard. He had a story to tell and it was not suitable for the ears of a child.

Although I had seen Pola Negri several times during the last years of her life, we never met. Kosleck knew her well during World War II. Her starring years in Hollywood had concluded with the box-office disaster of her talkie debut, *A Woman Commands* ('32), but she was still a name to moviegoers worldwide and was to remain an icon among homosexuals of Martin's generation. In 1943 when she made an attempted come-back in *Hi Diddle Diddle*, she leased 10051 Cielo Drive, the former estate of her one-time lover, Valentino. It was the setting for what Kosleck had to tell me.

"Dritcherd, even then I had no expectations of grandchildren, but vun vants to have tales to tell by the fireside." Apart from knowing many of the same people, he and La Negri enjoyed conversing in German. She and Martin spent a lot of time together while she was making the film opposite Menjou. One day at the end of shooting, he drove her to Falcon Lair to find that a fan had sent a magnum of Mumms, which her housekeeper had placed on ice.

"Bubbly ees my undoing, Dritcherd, because vun thing led to another. Zere ve ver, just the two of us in the house Valentino built. Ve played records and danced as long as ve could stand. Zen it happened. 'Vunderbar!' she said. Even better than Rudy had been. All I could think of vas either this vooman is an even greater actress than she vas on the screen or she didn't know any better. Maybe such awkward, drunken sex vas all she'd ever experienced."

I thought that entirely possible because the great vamp's last decades were spent with a wealthy Texan woman. Kosleck was well aware of this, but had never heard what I then told him, what perhaps only I could tell him. Over the years I had made a point of asking each of Rudolph Valentino's co-stars and leading ladies if they had been attracted to him. Doris Kenyon, Lois Wilson, Patsy Ruth Miller, Carmel Myers and Vilma Banky all liked him as an actor and a person, but they were not among the millions who swooned over his fabled sex appeal. Both of his wives, the actress Jean Acker and the dancer-designer Natacha Rambova, lived with women for many years until the ends of their lives. Dorothy Revier, who as the first lady of Columbia Pictures earned the unofficial title of "Queen of Poverty Row," had rehearsed and made a screen test opposite Valentino for *The Hooded Falcon*, which was cancelled upon his death. She told me she found him charming and professional, but that he did not appeal to her romantically.

Before we left, Stanton asked Martin to autograph the still of him I had brought along. In it, he was in full fig as Nazi propaganda minister Dr. Goebbels, complete with swastika armband. "Zis again," he remarked resignedly when I took it out of an envelope. "I'm always tempted to write on it vat he zeems to be zaying: 'Heil Hitler!' Isn't life filled vit irony? I vas born in Chermany, but I don't feel a bit Cherman."

His Russian father died when he was a young boy, having left Europe in 1931, his claim, never to have met a Nazi ("Except for Otto Preminger"), rang true.

Stanton was given some of the shortbread to take home and pronounce "A beautifully mannered young man who is velcome anytime at out home." The ten-year-old's comment as we drove away was "They're a couple, aren't they?"

Amidst the antiques to be found in and throughout the Kosleck-Drake bungalow were photos of the important women in Martin's life. Although they were no longer in touch, Marlene Dietrich was his first sponsor when they arrived in Hollywood almost simultaneously. Through her he had met Richard Cromwell. Through him he had begun a friendship with Bette Davis, which lasted until her death. The picture that most interested me, however, was a two-shot of Martin and Chris taken shortly after they met in 1948. The exact date was June 28. Forty years to the day later, I was invited to join them for a small celebration of their anniversary. Chris baked the ham, which was to be their entrée, on the previous day, so it could be served cold. The only other guests were to be the two guys who lived next door. They were bringing potato salad, which the celebrants hoped would be cold because the weather was so hot. "Ve zink it vil be the Cherman kind," commented Kosleck wearily, "because they insist it is my favorite. Vat can you do?" Seven o'clock is at least two hours earlier than I am used to having dinner, and I do not eat red meat. I left as the neighbors came bearing the salad and a couple of bottles of Korbel's Brut.

As I closed the gate to the front yard behind me, Martin called from the porch, "Champagne! God knows vut might happen."

All I ever learned of the remainder of their evening was that it went on until 11:30 pm, which they insisted had confused and upset their cats that were used to the lights being out by ten o'clock at the latest.

During my stay, Kosleck, urged and prompted by his companion, told me of what had transpired four decades before, at just about that very hour.

In the late forties, The Blue Angel was the "in" spot on the Sunset Strip for their crowd. One paid a bit more for a drink there than elsewhere, but you were buying safety from the very aggressive LAPD's vice squad. That part of West Hollywood was policed by the deputies of the sheriff of Los Angeles County rather than the city. The Strip was the hub of illegal activities such as prostitution, gambling and gay clubs that were as often as not referred to as "queer bars" by their patrons as well as public officials.

The Koslecks had dropped into The Blue Angel on that particular evening for an aperitif before going to dinner a few blocks west at the Cock 'N' Bull, a pub-like restaurant known as "The Home of the Moscow Mule," the drink that popularized vodka among post-World War II Americans.

"Eleanora knew vat vas my cup of tea, Dritcherd," said Martin.

Smartly dressed women with European accents and all the confidence a title, stage experience and a family fortune confers were exalted, fawned over in such a place as The Blue Angel. That generation of homosexual revered male flesh first and foremost, but a close second was glamour/sophistication, especially of the continental kind. The Baroness was not only wearing a veil, she smoked through it.

Christopher Drake, in his mid-twenties, was what was then referred to as a "queen's dream," an American version of Jean Marais, one of France's biggest stars and almost a rage among those whose type he was. He was wearing a sleeveless argyle sweater and his thick blond hair in a pompadour, the actor's trademark look.

Drake, an avid filmgoer, had spotted Martin about the same time the actress had seen him. The couple, after a quick rehearsal, went into their act. Kosleck, very nonchalantly, made his way to the men's room through the bar while she pretended to be looking for a public telephone. As he passed Chris, his heart pounding, he was asked "Aren't you a movie star?"

"No," he replied. "But I'm a movie actor."

By the time Martin had exited the john, Mrs. Kosleck and Drake were in animated conversation.

"Ve met cute, as Billy Wilder would zay," remarked the storyteller. "You zee my vife introduced me to my husband."

As our laughter subsided, I noticed that in order to lift his goblet of rosé, Martin had to use both hands. The fingers on his left hand were by then only slightly more mobile that his right.

The Baroness Mendelssohn had committed suicide, but not out of jealousy because her husband went off with a man.

"Ve married because ve cared deeply about each other," he told me. "I vould have loved to have seen Eleanora happy."

"So would I," interjected Chris.

"She vas delighted for us. My ship came in. She believed hers sank, I guess. Who knows? It vasn't all crying on each other's shoulders. Ve had lots of goot times, vit much laugher. Sometimes ve'd laugh about out crying. You zee actors love to act."

Another German-born actor I saw from time-to-time was Kurt Kreuger, who, because of his blond good looks, frequently played a love interest, albeit, as often as not, in a Nazi uniform. When I told Kosleck Krueger had sent him greetings, he reminded me that during World War II, when they were both busy playing Hitler's henchmen, Kurt claimed at times to be Dutch and, on other occasions, identified himself as Swiss. When asked once in a social situation about his countrymen's nationality, Martin replied that they had played together as children on the streets of Liechtenstein. This got back to Kreuger, who was not amused.

It was Kurt, however, who told me that Eleanor von Mendelssohn, whom he referred to as "the Baroness," had been addicted to either opium or morphine, he wasn't certain which, and that it was Kosleck who got her off the narcotic.

It came to me that Jean Marais was reputed to have performed the same service for his mentor-lover, Jean Cocteau.

While I was guesting on a KABC talk show one afternoon in 1988, a listener called in to say that she had recently viewed *Jezebel* ('38) on television and asked me to tell her whatever I could about the "startlingly handsome" young actor who played Henry Fonda's brother, Richard Cromwell. To help the radio audience put a face to the name of the long dead actor, I stated that he had also been leading man to Marie Dressler in *Emma* ('32) and Clara Bow in *Hoopla* ('33). In *Young Mr. Lincoln* ('39), Henry Fonda, playing the future president, defends him successfully against a murder charge.

During a commercial break, the producer passed me a message that had been phoned in. Someone name Opal Putnam asked that I call her. She was Richard Cromwell's sister, wanting to thank me for saying what I had about her brother. Since I had known him and sounded as though I liked Richard, perhaps I would like to come by sometime. She had all of his career memorabilia and some of his artwork.

Together one afternoon Mrs. Putnam and I went through dozens of photographs of Richard Cromwell and the scrapbooks she had kept from the day he was "discovered." I saw the column by Louella O. Parsons in which her younger brother was hailed as "Hollywood's Cinderella Man." The life masks she showed me I had seen twenty-eight years before except for those of Ann Sothern and Lilyan Tashman, a major theatrical personality and fashion plate of her time, the early thirties.

Opal and he had been the oldest of five. Their father, who had designed and built the Monoflyer, one of the most popular thrill rides at the Long Beach Pike, was one of the 21,000,000 who died from the Spanish Influenza that swept the world at the end of World War I. She and Richard had been ten and eight years old respectively at the time. They had always been especially close. To make her point, she went into her bedroom, returning with a photograph of brother and sister taken just after he had completed *This Day and Age* ('33) under Cecil B. De Mille's direction. Never would she forget the time he had burst into their family home proclaiming what had just happened. Not only had he just met his absolute favorite movie star, Joan Crawford, but we were going to a big party at her house. That is, she invited him and a date.

Before me was a professionally taken candid photo in a bakelite frame of two beautiful young people with an obvious bond between them absolutely ebullient with the joy on an evening long ago. Then Mrs. Putnam had a bit of a cry.

I was asked, whenever I spoke publicly again of Richard Cromwell, to let his fans know that, at the time of his passing, he had just been offered a one-man show at a Los Angeles art gallery owned by the actor Raymond Burr. Even more remarkable, he had actually signed to make his first picture since 1948, but had to withdraw when his condition worsened.

Kosleck well recalled how fond his friend was of his older sister and how attentive she had been when he got really sick. Then I repeated that she had told me one of the greatest thrills of her brother's life was an invitation from Gary Cooper to be one of his guests when the star's Duesenberg was raced in competition with Clark Gable's same model, the SSJ, in a race reported around the world. Martin and Chris fell about laughing.

"Tell him, tell him," Drake urged but his companion went instead for a Darvon to ease the pain spasms his laughter had triggered.

Taking over for him, Chris told me that the race wasn't the only time Gary Cooper had Richard very excited. Much of the picture they made together, *Lives of a Bengal Lancer* ('35), was shot on location in the desert. From the first day of filming, Cromwell felt certain both of his co-stars were on to him, but they were also friendly, and he sensed nothing judgmental. The other, Franchot Tone, he believed, kidded Cooper about the crush Richard had on him. Because of the heat, he said Gary was frequently in a state of partial undress. Either he was stripped to the waist or his robe was coming open. "Lucky no ladies are around" was Cooper's line at such times. Frequently when he came upon them, Gary would do one of his famous silent takes in which he seemed to project a big bashful country boy saying "Shucks!" It always broke Tone up. Funny as it sounded in the telling, at the time, it had been disconcerting to say the least. Frequently Cooper would call "Good morning" or "Good night" from the doorway of his trailer in his undershorts. All Richard could think was how lucky Lupe Velez and the Countess Di Frasso were.

According to Kosleck, his friend "dined out" for the rest of his life on his misadventures during the making of *Lives of a Bengal Lancer*. Someone at one dinner party, after listening to his routine, said he should have bade the star farewell at the movie's wrap party by telling him: "Gary, I've been having all these dreams and in them you're the star. Super-duper, Mr. Cooper!"

I said, and both Martin and Chris agreed, that the star would have known exactly what he was being told, would probably have been amused and have played the scene with the same visage Cromwell described. It has been my experience that good-looking straight actors are pleased to accept attention, any attention, from any quarter that could be construed as a compliment. They may not wish to have sex with homosexuals, but they want homosexuals to want to have sex with them.

The last time I saw Martin, Chris was out doing their grocery shopping and he was alone with their clutter of cats. He had me remove a few cubes of ice from a tray for his drink because he couldn't manage it. Without being asked, I carried his glass of Dubonnet into the living room.

"I veel zo helpless at times," he let out as we seated ourselves. "Dritcherd, I can't button or unbutton my clothes anymore. Thank God for Chris."

I told him of the recent talk I had had with the agent who had gotten Richard Cromwell what would have been his final screen role, the one he was too sick to accept. He was, he told me, a "hard sell." Someone at a casting office had described him as resembling an "old adolescent."

Martin allowed that his friend had always been rather conflicted, probably because he had been yanked from a profession to which he was quite dedicated, and made prominent, almost overnight, in another very different one. He didn't believe Richard, as much as he like the adulation and perks that went with movie acting, ever got used to it and then was unable to adjust to the fact that it was over.

He did, however, give himself over wholeheartedly to his craft of tile making, and then there was the long-running affair Cromwell had with an LAPD officer, who was married with four children. Kosleck and Drake had dinner with the family of six in the Miller Drive house several times. The kids were too young to catch on, and the wife impressed them as being hopelessly naïve.

"Dritcherd, I am the vun who vas supposed to be the decadent European, but it vus my very American friend who vus involved in this relationship right out of the last days of the Weimer. Life in Hollyvood!" remarked my host wryly as he reached for the long stem glass on the coffee table. Even after using both hands to bring it to his lips, there was the matter of their slight trembling. But the goblet was gold-rimmed and he was surrounded by silk and satin pillows and the creature beside him could have been a black panther's kitten. Pain, infirmity and advanced years had slowed this queen, but he was still grand and quite capable of enjoying a drink and a laugh and never failed to roll each and every one of his r's. And, as befits a queen, he had a consort, one who, even in his mid-sixties, bore unmistakable signs of the hunk he had once been. Although the first thing Martin had told Chris back then in The Blue Angel was that he was merely a movie actor, Drake gave his companion star treatment until the day he died in January 1994.

Chris survived him by only a few years. When I last visited him I pulled my car up in front of 1026 North Laurel Avenue to discover that only the house's roof and upper windows were visible from the street. The trees, shrubs, and vines were in such splendiferous bloom that I didn't need to ask how he was spending his time now that he no longer had to care for his late companion, who near the end was unable to even bathe himself. The living room furniture had been rearranged and recovered without Martin's discerning and precise eye.

After taking in all the changes of hues and fabrics, I said to my host, imitating our late friend, "But zis room is too dark for puce and vun never, ever uses two very different brocades. And, vy vould anyvun re-upholster in mohair vit cats about?"

Drake smiled, but somewhat sadly. Everything, including me, reminded him of the man whose life he had shared for over forty-five years. I, too, missed the presence of the somewhat perverse, pixilated Martin Kosleck.

Our mutual acquaintance, De Witt Bodeen, was fond of repeating the quip of Frances Marion, one of the most prominent scenarists of filmdom's golden age, on Hollywood relationships: "The only happy couples I've ever known in this town were Vilma Banky/Rod La Rocque and William Haines/Jimmy Shields."

When I quoted this as Chris walked me to my car, I could tell he didn't get my implication because he responded, "We never knew her."

"And, obviously, she never knew the two of you," I replied. A huge smile slowly came over his face, but, sensing tears were close behind, I started my motor. After closing the chain link gate to the front yard, still smiling, he waved.

I called my last words through the open window on the passenger's side: "And a rose garden, too!"

Up and Coming

Perhaps because I came of age in Hollywood, arriving when I was still in my teens, I tend to remember movie personalities of the fifties, not in the parts they played but, as how they looked and what they were doing when I encountered them. I saw *The High and The Mighty* (1954) and *Friendly Persuasion* (1956), both of which feature John Smith, but in my mind he will always be the very blond heartstopper in black tie with the starlet Karen Sharpe on his arm at the world premier of *A Star is Born* in 1954. A year or so later I was lunching alfresco at Frascati's across from the Beverly Wilshire Hotel when he pulled to the curb in front and stepped out of a lipstick-red Oldsmobile convertible, top back, of course.

Only in Tinseltown could a name such as John Smith garner publicity. It was changed from Robert Van Orden by his agent Henry Willson, who was well known within the profession for discovering extraordinarily good-looking young actors and re-christening them with monikers such as Rock Hudson, Tab Hunter, Race Gentry, Ford Dunhill and Troy Donahue.

When Wilson introduced his discovery to the press he pointed out that he had chosen "John Smith" to prove that a client with such looks and talent needed no gimmick to stand apart from the many other young actors. The ploy worked and throughout his career, which lasted over ten years, the handsome actor's stock reply to anyone who brought up the blandness of his assumed name was, "So how many John Smiths do you know?"

Eventually I would have surely gotten around to including him in one of my *Whatever Became of...?* books, but while guesting on KFMB in San Diego late one night in early 1987, everything fell right into place. A

John Smith.

female listener called in to ask what had happened to the handsome hunk who appeared on the "TV show *Cimarron City* in the late fifties?" She was a teenager when it was on the air and had a crush on him. I responded, "I'll take the case. Next time I'm on this program, ask me again."

"You're very sure of yourself," quipped my host Bill Balance. "Is it really all that easy?" For me it was because all I needed to do was contact Smith's ex-wife, Luana Patten, the former Walt Disney contractee. I had profiled her in my eighth book and knew their divorce had been amicable and that they had stayed in touch.

It was, however, more complicated than I had anticipated because Smith's telephone had been disconnected. This, his ex-spouse explained, had happened before but as soon as it was working again, he was sure to call her with the new number, which she would then pass on to me. They had recently had coffee together after she had pulled to a stop at a red light and spotted him seated on a bus bench. His driving license had been revoked several years before. That was all Luana Patten told me, and I got the picture.

By then I was working with the doyen of Hollywood autograph hounds, Marty Jackson, who always snapped photos of the celebrities he met. Since I prefer not to have anyone along when I conduct interviews, he and I usually saw my subjects separately. As a nonprofessional, Marty never called beforehand to make an appointment with the personality. He earned his living as a delivery man for a florist, which allowed him to stop off to get his book signed whenever he was in the areas where notables lived. Once they had been photographed, I could get all the information I required over the telephone. I might, therefore, never have met John Smith had Jackson not gone by himself to the address Luana Patten had given me and experienced what he did.

Autograph collecting had been his hobby since he was fourteen years old, so he had seen famous people under highly unusual circumstances. In April 1972, when Charles Chaplin returned to his bungalow at the Beverly Hills Hotel holding the Oscar he had accepted an hour before, Marty was there waiting for him. He had been sitting across from luminaries when they came out from under anesthesia in their hospital rooms and as they left the State Office of Unemployment. In his own way, my colleague was very sophisticated as to the various lifestyles and behavior patters of screen personalities from Pickfair to trailer parks and halfway houses. Until his death at the age of forty-six in 2003, however, Jackson maintained he had never encountered anything even approaching what he had that day on Crenshaw Boulevard. By the eighties, the area had become a solidly middle-class black neighborhood with the exception of John Smith, who was residing in the one-story frame house in which he had grown up.

I was waiting to hear from Luana Patten with Smith's new telephone number, but Marty didn't need it. One afternoon after taking a wreath to a funeral home a few blocks away, he pulled his truck up in front of the address I had shared with him.

It was quite a warm day and two elderly women were seated side by side chatting in the swing on the porch next door. He felt he had their attention while walking up the pathway and ringing the front doorbell. Waiting for an answer, he smiled and nodded at the neighbors who appeared to be in amused anticipation. After three rings he was about to leave, but one of the ladies called over, "Dey be home. You need to knock, too." Knock he did and rang several more times, but there was no response. As he came down the steps the same woman pointed to the rear of the property. He could hear her and her companion tee-heeing as he made his way up the driveway. The door of the garage was open, but it was empty. Walking a few more yards Marty discovered the residents. A fiftyish woman was slumped, head between her legs, on the top step to the porch. A male figure he took to be John Smith was face down just off the cement walkway. As Jackson put it, "I guess he made it onto the lawn, although there wasn't any grass in the backyard, just dirt and weeds. Better, I guess than passing out on the concrete or asphalt."

His presence appeared to revive the woman who, once conscious, was actually welcoming although she had no idea who he was or why he was there. With their visitor's help she and Marty managed to get the man of the house through the side door and upright on the living room couch. The rear entrance was blocked by cardboard cartons piled almost to the ceiling.

Just as soon as names were exchanged, he was offered a cold drink with the proviso that he bring one for each of them because, as Smith said, "Neither of us can make it that far."

There were no beverages on ice, except beer. In fact there was very little in the refrigerator but six-packs with several cases of same stacked alongside it. At some point it was explained to him that he had arrived shortly after they returned from grocery shopping. The cab driver had helped them bring in everything they bought, mostly Budweiser, after which, said Smith's companion, "Johnny and I, we were all tuckered out."

The woman's name was Ruth. Neither she nor Smith ever inquired as to why he was there. At one point, however, John Smith turned to her and asked, "Nice to have some company for a change, isn't it?"

An hour or so later when Jackson left, he had been invited to return "real soon" and to bring along the person he mentioned because it would be great to have a picture of the three of them together now that they were such good friends. Anytime was fine with John and Ruth because they were nearly always at home. He exited with both their autographs because Ruth claimed that she had been married to the son of the character actor Edward G. Robinson as well as being a former Miss Ohio.

Marty phoned me as soon as he returned to his apartment, with news of his adventure. When I suggested he give me the whole story over dinner, he declined by saying, "What I have to tell you doesn't go good with food." Perhaps to gradually prepare me for what was coming, he told me that the table and chairs in the dining room of the Smith residence were piled high with bedding, towels and articles of clothing. Responding to my question as to whether or not they had been washed, he said, "Richard, nothing and no one in that house had been washed in a long time." Furthermore, before leaving, he had used the bathroom and found the tub overflowing with still more soiled laundry and the interior of the toiled bowl the color of what he described as "nicotine brown." But the "Killer," as Marty called it, was what drew and held his attention on the coffee table as the three sat sipping from sixteen-ounce cans of Bud. In its center was a large ashtray containing ashes, many burnt matches, and countless cigarette butts. Among them was matter that, for a while at least, his conscious mind refused to accept as possible, but his eyes kept returning to it. "Oh, Gawd!" moaned his host when he noticed what their guest was staring at. "That otta've been attended to long before this."

"He means that *I* should've thrown it out," was Ruth's playful response. Neither, however, stirred.

Marty Jackson often showered twice daily. He frequently flossed his teeth. Unable to bear it any longer, he offered to empty it all into the toilet. But, Smith proclaimed, "We're both of us heavy smokers." He was concerned that it might clog the plumbing and asked him to throw the contents in what he referred to as the "trash" in the kitchen. The problem, however, for Marty was what might be considered in their home to be refuse because the floor around the stove, fridge and sink was absolutely covered in bags, empty food containers, boxes and overflowing receptacles.

"Bring us a couple of cold ones while you're out there" called the actor. "And get another for yourself."

"We could use Marty around here, couldn't we, Johnny?" quipped Ruth as Jackson returned with two tall boys and the empty ashtray. He was still somewhat shaken by what he had disposed of and wanted to assure me that the Smith home had no pets and to remind me that they had been seated in the living room. In the center of the ashes, burnt match sticks and cigarette stubs but by no means buried by them was, well, he had been brought up to refer to it as "number two."

Once it was disposed of, although by no means erased from his mind, he might even have had a second beer if Ruth hadn't done what she did. While proceeding to brush off the dirt that clung to her companion's shirt, it fell open. What followed greatly unnerved their guest who then made the excuse that his mother was expecting him home for supper.

"You'll pardon us for not seeing you to the door, buddy," were John Smith's parting words. "But, as you can see we're kinda busy just now. Ruthie really loves to do this." The hostess looked up long enough from licking and sucking the actor's nipple to say, "Yeah, I sure do. Hurry back, Marty."

On the following Sunday Jackson, accompanied by a friend, a western enthusiast who revered the actor for his leading role on the TV series *Laramie* from 1959 to 1963, returned to the bungalow on Crenshaw Boulevard for an autograph-photo session. Both of the couple were friendly, cooperative and appeared sober during the visit that took place in the early afternoon.

Days later, Luana Patten rang me to say that her ex-husband once again had a working telephone. She had just spoken with him and he was expecting to hear from me, seemed to be looking forward to it.

Jackson accompanied me when I interviewed John Smith a week or so later in June 1987 because by then he had prints of the shots he had taken of him with Ruth. The couple had no pictures of themselves together and had been anxious to see how they turned out.

On our way there Marty allowed that there was one thing he had left out about the Smith house. He was eager to watch the expression on my face when I saw it and was in a state of bemused anticipation.

It was, however, Marty who got the day's biggest surprise.

Smith greeted us through the *oeil-de-boeuf* in the front door, asking that we give him a minute to get his clothes on. We had arrived on the dot of two o'clock, as agreed, but he was running a few minutes late, and had just stepped out of the shower. As he walked away to get dressed, I got a good look at his naked backside. Alcohol and the years had taken their toll on his face and, no doubt, his insides, but his ass was pink and firm as if he was twenty-five years old.

After the door was opened a minute or two later by a completely sober, neatly dressed fifty-seven year old, we were invited into a shabbily furnished, but tidy and clean house.

The shocker, however, for Jackson came when he presented the color shots of John and Ruth taken only a few weeks before. We were informed that two or three days afterward Smith had turned over in bed one morning to find Ruth Conte lying beside him dead. For a moment, I thought he was going to break down in tears while he told us how much she had anticipated seeing the color two-shots.

Marty got himself a beer, but I declined, as did Smith who was "on the wagon," as he put it.

When we stood to leave almost two hours later, I asked the question that had been foremost in my mind since I entered. "About the hole here in your wall, I can't help but wonder…"

Laughing, he admitted that he had been hoping I wouldn't notice. It was hardly something one would miss. About the size of a ship's porthole, it had been broken through with a hammer from the living room into the master bedroom as a convenience for the residents by the homeowners. The aperture permitted anyone reclining on the couch to speak with whoever was lying in bed without raising his or her voice or getting up. The house rule was that the person in the living room, thereby being closest to the kitchen, was obliged to get the cold Buds from the fridge and pass one through on request. Now that Smith was living by himself it served no purpose and would be patched up "One of these days when I get around to it."

"Ruthie and me, we got along really well together," he mused as we made our exit. "It's sure nice to have these pictures, Marty, and to meet you, Richard. Luana spoke so highly of you. I'll be thinking about all the people and times your questions brought to mind for days and days. You mentioned that I dated Terry Moore and Venetia Stevenson, but I took out Phyllis Gates, too. She went from being my agent's secretary to Mrs. Rock Hudson. John Smith was 'up-and-coming' then. That's what they called me in the fan magazines. 'Up-and-coming'."

Whoever Heard of Jean Malin?

Movie Star News, situated between Second and Third Avenues up one flight at 212 East 14 Street, received little walk-in trade. Most of its business was done through the mails. Despite its name and a vast stock of motion picture stills, what were sold mainly were "girlie shots," as semi-nude and fetish photos were then known in the trade. When the Hollywood memorabilia craze hit in the late sixties, sales soared. Still, no screen personality was to outsell the ever-popular Betty Page, undisputed queen of the pin-ups.

Her many fans sent in their checks from around the world along with discreetly worded requests for the black-banged beauty modeling bathing suits, lingerie, leather and rubber gear as well as other "provocatives."

By the time I began going to Movie Star News to buy portraits for my first book, the founder, Irving Klaw, had died, leaving it to his niece, Paula.

The proprietress was usually to be found just inside the front door behind a counter. Even when seated, it was apparent that she was an exceptionally large woman. As though to emphasize her height of, at least, six feet, she wore her hair in a beehive. As large as her body was, her head still seemed over-size, making her appear top-heavy. No matter how many times I encountered her, Paula Klaw's appearance never failed to startle me.

Regulars were allowed to wander about at will to search through dusty cartons, boxes and metal file cabinets so antiquated they had no rollers on their drawers. Before the history of motion pictures was even taken seriously, much less taught in universities, one could meet experts in almost every aspect of film-making as they rummaged through the hundreds of thousands of stills in the archive-like setting. They were always males, my age and older, people whose lives and personalities had been shaped mainly by Hollywood-made films. Some, appreciative that I was interviewing the screen personalities of yesteryear each week on radio, introduced themselves and offered assistance and suggestions.

One wintry afternoon, as I stomped the slush from my rubbers on the door mat, Paula called out into the stacks, "Mr. Robbins, you wanted to meet Richard Lamparski. Here he is."

The fiftyish man who came forward had about him the aura of someone with a very sweet nature seconded by a rather dark karma. There was one of him in every fraternity house, club and bar. He was the guy who played the piano well and gladly and who frequently stood treat for drinks.

John Robbins had been from birth the apple of his wealthy grandfather's eye and was the heir to much of the old man's fortune. A large part of that money had gone to lawyers after he was convicted of second-degree murder shortly after V-J Day. The attorney who handled the appeals on his case could have gotten Robbins out long before 1956, had his client not adamantly refused to admit his guilt.

"I didn't kill anyone and I didn't commit perjury," he told the parole board every time he came before them. "I'm not going to lie to you now. I am innocent. Not 'not guilty.' *Innocent.*"

After eleven years in New York State's prison system, John Robbins was released. I never sensed any bitterness about the incarceration and more that once heard him say that it had saved his life.

"I was a complete lush," he told me. "Had I been free all that time I'd have drunk myself to death long before now. For me, the worst part was that cons were only shown one movie a month."

John went to one or two films daily, seeing most of the new releases and, eventually, all of those he missed while behind bars.

Like myself, he was more drawn by the players than the pictures they were in and had a remarkable memory for their careers and private lives, as were reported in the press of the time. From the day we met, he became my unpaid assistant. Whenever I was set to interview a screen personality of the past, I had only to call John, who could usually give me their credits, marriages and romances off the top of his head. For dates, obscure titles and billing, he had only to consult one or more of the many books on cinema he owned.

John Robbins ate out every meal. When he leased a studio apartment in the Sutton East Hotel, the management removed the stove and refrigerator, thus enabling its new tenant to keep his vast library, still and record collection in what had theretofore served as the kitchen.

The contents of the large alcove spilled far into the main room. Over its entrance there was a hand-painted sign that read "My Reel Life." When we first met, John had lived in the same L-shaped room for about 10 years. Although he was entitled to have it re-painted periodically, it never had been. This was because on top of the chock-full cabinets and cases there were boxes, 11x14 portrait albums, stacks of sheet music, lobby cards, and magazines. Very little of the wall was visible. What one could see, as well as the ceiling, was stained the yellow-brown of nicotine from the Camels he smoked incessantly.

It took such a cineaste as he to come up with what for me was the definitive description of Paula Klaw. Without exaggeration or malice, he said she resembled "Rondo Hatton* in drag."

My relationship with John Robbins, which was to continue until his death from lung cancer in 1987, was as ironic and surprise-filled as any I've ever experienced.

One of the first things I discovered was that of all the personalities of twenties Hollywood, the one he most wanted to meet was Aileen Pringle, star of the silents made from the Elinor Glyn best-sellers *Three Weeks* ('24) and *His Hour* ('24). It was with the title of another of her novels, "*It*," that she named and defined the quality that to millions around the world came to mean a combination of sex appeal, glamour, charisma and "that certain something." Studio publicists trumpeted Clara Bow as the "It Girl," but it was La Pringle whom Mme. Glyn first proclaimed to possess "It."

Of all the celebrities I was acquainted with, I had known Aileen Pringle the longest and the most intimately. Furthermore, she lived less than two blocks from the front door of the Sutton East. The rub was that we had been out of touch for over seven years. She was someone from my past I had no intention of ever seeing again, even as a guest on my radio program. I found the nearness of that miss and the reason it was so utterly out of question to be somewhat unsettling.

But John had other favorites and one was Jacqueline Logan, who had played Mary Magdalene under Cecil B. De Mille's direction in *King*

---

* Rondo Hatton (1895-1946) played "The Creeper" in the "Sherlock Holmes" feature *Pearl of Death* ('44), *The Spider Woman Strikes Back* ('46), and *The Brute Man* ('46). His skull, facial features, hands and feet were enlarged and distorted by the disease acromegaly.

of Kings ('27). Only a few months before he and I met, she had given me a birthday luncheon party at a creekside French restaurant near her home in Bedford Hills, New York. When I told him the other guests were her contemporaries, Leatrice Joy, Dagmar Godowsky, Lina Basquette, Patsy Ruth Miller, and Lois Wilson, Robbins was amazed that these women, stars when he was in prep school, were recently together and that someone he knew was present.

Never mind that all that remained of Jacqueline Logan's once staggering beauty were the enormous blue-green eyes. He didn't care that she was now a gray-haired matron and an ardent member of the John Birch Society. One of the heroines of his youth had served him tea and homemade cookies before her huge stone fireplace. A dream had come true and there was an autographed portrait and a set of snapshots of them together to prove it. The other collectors at Movie Star News would be green with envy.

The Sutton East at 330 East 56 Street was mostly residential and more that a bit seedy. I remember someone at one of my friend Sunshine's soirees mentioning in passing that Nathanael West had been its night manager before he wrote *Miss Lonely Hearts* or *Day of the Locust*. I learned later that the novelist's father was its owner. Dorothy Parker had lived there for a while, as had West's brother-in-law, and Dashiell Hammett.

Its ambiance was more likely to have inspired the latter's "Sam Spade" stories that those about the Thin Man. Neither Nick nor Nora Charles would have ever been caught in such a place, except, as the saying goes, "over somebody's dead body."

Robbins knew the building's history, but the part of it he told to first-time visitors was of Russell Gleason's death. In 1945 the thirty-six year old son of stage and screen actors James and Lucille Gleason "fell" from his fourth floor window of the Sutton East. Neither his parents nor the police ever disclosed further details.

Crime and glamour had a strong pull on John all of his life. I had never given much credence to genetic predisposition until he and I became friends. His parents had been very much part of the set referred to as the Lost Generation of the Roaring Twenties.

During 1930-1, while the Great Depression was beginning to take hold, they divorced and John came into his money. His father, Tod Robbins, moved to France, intending to revive what some had looked upon as a promising career as a writer. It was one of his stories, *Spurs*, published in

1923, that provided the basis for the controversial film *Freaks** ('32).

His son for a few years became part of his mother's world. The ex-Mrs. Robbins, a beauty pageant winner, was a member of what was known as Café Society. Then he lived for a while on the West Coast.

By early 1939, war jitters were being felt throughout Europe. Fearing it would be his last chance for a while to do so, John visited his father in Cannes. One evening that summer, someone he ran into from California took him to a bar that was whispered about throughout the Riviera. In it, males were sometimes allowed to dance together.

"Even on the decadent Cote d'Azur that sort of thing simply wasn't done," Robbins confided to me almost thirty years later in New York City, where it was still illegal.

"Come midnight, the prices of drinks doubled and someone stood watch in the doorway to the street, keeping an eye out for the gendarmes. As soon as the mulatto pianist began playing, a sailor from down Argentine way took my companion out onto the floor. Just then a type we used to call 'tall, dark and handsome' came out of the loo and asked me for a dance. I took him for another American, but he turned out to be from Canada. I'd never have given him another thought if I hadn't seen his picture plastered over every front page in New York a few years later. He was none other than Wayne Lonergan**, the number who beat his wife's head in with a candlestick when she bit his cock. At least that was the story going around at the time. There followed a long, ugly trial with all the dirt coming out about his rich father-in-law, whom he had hustled. That's how he met the daughter.

I was quite familiar with the case, which was still occasionally talked about in my circles. Lonergan had become involved with the victim's father, heir to a brewery fortune, after they met at the World's Fair in 1940. The younger man worked as a guide pushing the millionaire in a rolling chair throughout the various exhibits. Their relationship had concluded and the older man had died before the killing took place.

---

* The screenplay for *Freaks* ('32) was based on "Spurs;" a short story by Tod Robbins published in 1923 in *Munsey's Magazine*.

** Details of this case are to be found in an article by Dominic Dunne in the July 2000, *Vanity Fair*. Wayne Lonergan was twenty-seven and a member of the RCAF when he was found guilty of second-decree murder. This despite the prosecution's failure to show that he was at the scene of the crime or that he had handled the weapon. The confession police said he gave was neither authenticated nor signed by him. The defense argued that the accused lacked a motive, but the state managed to get before the jury testimony that Lonergan had once admitted to taking part in sexual orgies. After serving twenty-two years on a sentence of thirty years to life, he was paroled in 1965.

Convicted of second-degree murder, he served twenty-two years on a "33 to life" sentence.

Anticipating both of my questions, John volunteered the answers. Yes, he and Lonergan had been in Sing Sing at the same time, but they had never been face to face.

"Of course, if you had," I said, "your line would *have* to have been, 'shall we dance?'"

Robbins' favorite place for Italian food was the Original Joe's on East 59 Street. There was another restaurant around the corner on Third Avenue named Original Joe's, but he always maintained that where we went was the authentic one.

We hadn't yet even looked at our menus one evening in 1971 when, after the first sip of my Campari, I began telling John about the telephone call I had that day from Buster Davis, the musical director of the current Broadway hit, the revival of *No, No, Nanette*, staring Ruby Keeler.

We knew each other only by professional reputation. Davis had phoned at the insistence of a mutual acquaintance, the actor Don Koll. He was a regular listener to my radio program and knew I'd want to hear how Patsy Kelly* had gotten one of the leads in the hit musical. Koll had heard him tell the story at a party.

According to Davis, Cyma Rubin, one of the show's producers, had firmly vetoed the idea as soon as the name mentioned. She had heard for years that the comedienne was a problem drinker and thought "Patsy Kelly" on a marquee would mean virtually nothing to the theatre-going public.

A week before rehearsals were to begin, however, the company was still without someone to play Ruby Keeler's maid, the role Buster Davis thought Patsy Kelly perfect for. At a break during a last minute production meeting, he spotted someone backstage reading the first volume of *Whatever Became of...?*.

Borrowing the copy, he held it before Cyma Rubin and asked if she was familiar with it. The producer hadn't read it, but she knew there was such a book. She heard that guy who wrote it on Long John Nebel's late night radio show and was impressed.

That said, he read aloud from the page on which I had written of Patsy Kelly: "In 1955 she toured the country with her old friend Tallulah

---

* Patsy Kelly won the Tony award for the Best Supporting Actress in a Musical during the 1970-71 Broadway season.

Bankhead in the farce *Dear Charles*. Patsy was on stage no more than fifteen minutes, but at the final curtain she got as much applause as the star. When her movies appear on television after some thirty years TV magazines and newspapers often recommend an otherwise dated film with the comment: 'Worth watching for the Patsy Kelly scenes.'"

Even though I didn't know any of the personalities involved, it was a very nice feeling, being part of a tale with such a happy ending, especially because Patsy Kelly, as the saying goes, was great in the part.

Robbins smiled wistfully. From this expression, I guessed something in what he just heard had triggered his memory.

"Patsy Kelly," he began, slowly and thoughtfully. "I stood only a few yards from her one night, must be over thirty years ago. Everyone there thought she was a goner. I remember one of the firemen who lifted her on a stretcher shaking his head and telling one of the cops that not only had she nearly drowned, but that a lot of the water she'd swallowed was sandy."

There were things about what had occurred that he didn't know or couldn't understand, but John shared with me everything he could recall and what he had heard over the years. It was the first time I had ever heard the name Jean Malin.

As he was concluding I was walking him home along 57th Street. At his suggestion we continued on to the pocket park at Sutton Place. Robbins wanted me to visualize what he and a handful of others had witnessed late at night long before in the waves of the Pacific Ocean.

"What a fade-out!" I exclaimed after I heard it. It was a Hollywood ending to an "Only in Hollywood" happening. All I had to do was fill in the dates and details and talk with others who knew those involved. It took over twenty years of viewing microfilms, reading yellowed clippings, and conducting interviews, plus several generous dollops of what some call "luck."

As soon as Billy Livingstone heard the name of the central figure in the story he lit up. It was set in what he always referred to as "My period."

"Leave it to you to come up with Jean Malin," cried the tiny Texan costume designer. "Darlin', that whole thing just knocked everyone I knew in the business for a loop. What happened and how. And just when he was about to make it in pictures. Did your friend tell you the word around was that they were going to put him opposite Mae West? Like they did later with W. C. Fields."

Billy phoned his friend Betty Kean on my behalf. I knew her sister, Jane, but this was one of the frequent periods when the Kean Sisters, as they were known professionally, weren't on speaking terms. Betty and Patsy Kelly had palled around for years, and she promised to get us together as soon as the national tour of *No, No, Nanette* ended.

"Funny thing about Patsy Kelly," Billy remarked. "She's not a bit funny. She knows there's something about her that makes people laugh, but it beats her as to what it is. I understand Bert Lahr's the same way."

He then began to tell me about his recent visit to New Orleans. His host in the French Quarter, the flamboyant antique dealer Elmo, had taken him to a cocktail party Tennessee Williams threw for himself in a recently vacated mortuary. But he interrupted himself to ask, "You do know, don't you, that there were *three* sudden deaths in Patsy's career? Only a few years after Jean there was Thelma Todd's* murder. Patsy wasn't under suspicion, but they were working together when someone did her in. They've still not solved that one. Then a real looker of a blonde, Polish I think, named Lyda Roberti** had just been teamed with Patsy when she dropped dead. Believe me, three in a row like that gets you a bad rep. You know how they are in this town. 'What is it with this dyke? She jinxed or something?'"

As soon as Patsy Kelly had settled into an apartment a few floors above Betty Kean's in the Hollywood Ardmore on N. Whitley, the three of us met over drinks.

Patsy Kelly and I had many mutual acquaintances and were getting on very well when I brought up Jean Malin.

"O, God!" she said clasping her breast. "I can't talk about that. It was like when Lyda fell over dead. It made no sense. All I could think was they wanted another angel up there. But it still hurts to even think of either of them. I just don't want to go into any of it."

Turning to our hostess she asked, "Betty, did you ever know Jean? Ever see him work? There was no one like him. Maybe Liberace now. But Jean was damn good looking on top of it. He could compére- doncha love that word? That's what they call emceeing in Blighty-the end of the world and everyone would be saying 'Isn't this show fun?' But I just don't want

---

* The busty blonde was a foil for knockabout comics, both male and female. When she died mysteriously in 1935, she was partnered in "Thelma Todd's Sidewalk Café" at 17575 Pacific Coast Highway across from the Pacific Ocean. The "Ice Cream Blonde," as she was publicized, lived above the restaurant, and was rumored to have recently refused a proposal by crime czar Lucky Luciano that she front a gambling den on the property.

** In the book *They Had Faces Then*, by John Springer and Jack Hamilton, Lyda Roberti is described as "a sort of platinum blonde Lupe Velez (but more good-humored in her uninhibited pursuit of men)." She was working as a team with Patsy Kelly when the comedienne died of a heart attack in 1938. Lyda Roberti was in her apartment in Hollywood's Chateau Marmont and had just bent over to tie a shoelace. She was thirty-one years old.

to talk about him. Not even after the next drink, the one if madam doesn't mind, I'll help myself to."

Somewhat disappointing but not at all discouraging. Was I not the "Whatever Became of...?" man? I knew who else to ask about Jean Malin and I had their phone numbers.

Both Jack and Flo Haley remembered the dramatic ending, but had never caught his act.

The next day, Mrs. Haley phoned to say that after we hung up, Jack had recalled Lila Lee talking about Malin. I knew the actress' son, Jimmy Kirkwood* the novelist-playwright, and called him. He had his mother phone me.

A week or so after she and I spoke, a 1932 publicity photo arrived in the mail with the return address, "Lila Lee, Hotel Wyndham, NYC." In it, she is seated in the center of a banquette, smiling through a veil. On her right is Alexander Hall, who had just been assigned to direct Claudette

From left to right: movie director, Alexander Hall, leading lady, Lila Lee, and Jean Malin, photographed on December 5, 1932 in the Club New Yorker.

---

* Jimmy Kirkwood's novel, *There Must Be a Pony*, was published in 1960. In 1976, he shared a Tony Award and a Pulitzer Prize as co-author of *A Chorus Line*. His father, James Kirkwood, was a leading man in silent pictures and, reputably, Mary Pickford's first lover.

Colbert in *Torch Singer* ('33). The third figure, Jean Malin, is as husky and blond as he had been described. He is carefully groomed and there's a carnation in the lapel of his dinner jacket.

The instant Billy Livingston looked at the still, he was able to tell me where it had been taken. All he needed to see was the pair of shoes very stylistically painted on the wall over Malin's head.

"Henry Clive* did those, Darlin'," said my little friend. "He was one of the top illustrators of the day. Did a lot of magazine covers. He decorated a hot spot on Hollywood Boulevard with life-size dancing and prancing figures. For the life of me I can't think of what it was called. Jean's in a tux because he was working there. Made a big hit. Look at all the gold jewelry he's got on. And why not? By this time, he was a name on both coasts. He'd made it."

The Hollywood historian and archivist, Marc Wanamaker, confirmed where my picture of the trio had been taken. He was certain because the murals were still there, even though the Club New Yorker had been closed for over a decade. It was in the basement of what had once been the Hotel Christie on Hollywood Boulevard at McFadden Place. From his files, he gave me another 1932 photo. It was of the entrance and marquee showing "Jean Malin" in letters larger than the club's name. The singer Nick Lucas provided me with two straight males' reactions to Jean Malin.

"I saw him at a joint in the Village around '29 or '30," he recalled. "*Gold Diggers of Broadway* was in release and he asked me to stand up. You know how they do. The band played a few strains of 'Tip Toe through the Tulips'. It was a speakeasy. Very noisy with low ceilings and lots of smoke. Not an easy crowd to play to. He had an entrance line that was his signature, like Texas Guinan's 'Hello, Suckers!' Can't think of it. Anyway out he comes at one o'clock in the morning in a white suit, which made him look even bigger than he was. He walks onto the stage like it's his living room and barks out this line. Well, 'You're all under arrest!' would have had the same effect. He took charge right then and held it throughout.

"The fellow I was with and myself were dating girls who were in the show. When they told us later how much fun Jean was to work with, my buddy makes this face. You see Malin did a lot of swishy stuff that night, which, I guess, offended him. But, he agreed with me that this guy was going places. I'll tell you something, that could have been part of his shtick. A lot of people played fey. It got laughs. I remember when we met

---

* The artist was briefly married to Acquanetta, "The Venezuelan Volcano."

backstage, he shook my hand and his felt like Jack Dempsey's. Let's put it this way, all a guy built like that would have to do is fall on you and you'd be outta commission."

One newspaper account of Jean Malin's death claimed he had "one of the quickest tongues on Broadway," as well as an "unabashed effrontery" and "a cultivated lisp." It was accompanied by a photo taken in a Hollywood nitery showing Malin in white tie and tails. He is smiling broadly. The silent screen star Constance Talmadge is on his right side and the daughter-in-law of famed evangelist Billy Sunday on the other. Both are laughing heartily.

Hollywood's most famous drug store stood for many years on the southeast corner of Sunset Boulevard and Laurel Canyon. The gossip columnist Sidney Skolsky had his office on the mezzanine overlooking the lunch counter.

Another credited him with having created a "vogue for effeminacy with his crop of blond hair as thick as a $4 doormat and undulating hip."

Several reports mentioned that he had recently completed roles in two 1933 movies, *Arizona to Broadway* with Joan Bennett, and the Joan Crawford starrer *Dancing Lady*, but he is not in the release print of either.

After George Eells learned of my interest in Jean Malin, he dug through his files for a Sidney Skolsky article on him. He had come across it while researching his book *Hedda and Louella* and showed it to Mae West. Her comment was, "Just as he was taking off, the curtain fell."

One of the supposed signs of having arrived in Hollywood was being profiled by Skolsky. The piece he did on Jean Malin was a guaranteed attention-getter. The columnist had made, and maintained for years, a nation-wide reputation by asking everyone he interviewed very much the same set of questions. His regular readers must have been given a turn by the highly irregular answers he got from the twenty-three year old entertainer in 1931.

Malin said he slept in black silk pajamas, which he also wore while breakfasting in bed, something he did every morning. Bed was also where he had his weekly manicure. He bathed twice daily and used 4711 toilet water exclusively. His undershorts were also silk, and the ones he was wearing that day were blue and green.

But Malin couldn't simply be dismissed as a campy clothes horse, even after one read about his wardrobe of twenty-eight suits, sixteen pairs of shoes and "about 500" neckties. When asked about the wristwatch he had on, he revealed it was made of onyx and platinum, a gift from Lucille Malin, his wife.

The marriage rated a story with picture in the January 31, 1931 edition of the New York *Daily News* bannered "Jean Malin Marries Girl!" The groom was shown wearing an ankle length raccoon coat.

When I told this to John Robbins he said he was almost sure my friend Joe O'Donahue IV used to be seen around with her for years after Malin's death. It was again a case of confusing one playboy with another. O'Donahue acknowledged that he knew her, but only slightly: "She was one of Jimmy Donohue's intimates. She was a madam. Ran the next best whorehouse in New York City. The best was Polly Adler's*. Lu did not peddle males, only dazzling girls at astronomical prices."

---

* Polly Adler, the well-known madam of the twenties and thirties, wrote her autobiography, *A House is Not a Home*, which was published in 1953. It was filmed in 1963 with Shelly Winters in the starring role.

"Now hear me!" was what Jean Malin used to call out over the din of the speakeasies he performed in during Prohibition. He used the phrase along with a stylized drawing of himself on his Christmas card of 1932, months before his dramatic death by drowning.

Although she used a number of aliases whenever she was arrested, a frequent occurrence throughout the thirties and into the forties, the newspapers invariable referred to her as "Mrs. Lucille Malin, widow of Jean..."

Billy Livingston's companion added a postscript to their 1982 Christmas card: "I last saw Lucille about 12 years ago in NYC. She goes by another last name, but was still doing business on a small scale."

Virginia Cherill gave me another brief, but vivid glimpse of Jean Malin "on."

She was in New York and out for the evening with the man who eventually became her husband, Cary Grant. She couldn't remember the name of the nitery where they saw Malin, but his put-down of a celebrity was seared in her memory: "Peggy Hopkins Joyce* was what we would call today someone who is 'famous for being famous'. Much married. Always to serious money. Bejeweled and over-dressed. Anyway, she and one of the hubbies mad a grand entrance just as the emcee was introducing a number. As the captain led their party to a table ringside, she stopped here and there along the way to say "Hello!" Waved. Blew kisses. Very much the star, which of course she wasn't. My eyes were on her and the fur coat she was draped in. But Cary must have sensed an oncoming ad-lib because he nudged me to watch Malin, perfectly cool and collected, no matter how much he must have been fuming inside. Just as a waiter was pulling out a chair for her, this Malin booms, 'All right, dear, we've all seen the chinchilla. You may sit down now.' Well, everyone screamed, and he just let them. We all laughed and laughed and she looked like she wanted to crawl into a hole somewhere. Then, of course, the show proceeded, but Cary talked about the moment for days."**

Samson De Brier, the noted Hollywood host, eccentric and compul-

---

* Peggy Hopkins Joyce (1893-1957) was mentioned in the lyrics of Cole Porter's "Why Shouldn't I?" from *Jubilee* ('35) and "Let's Not Talk About Love" from *Let's Face It* ('41). Although she was featured by Flo Ziegfeld in a *Follies* and Earl Carroll in one of his *Vanities*, the actress is best remembered for her screen appearance in *International House* ('33) with W. C. Fields and as a celebrity of her times. Renowned for her beauty and the jewelry she eventually owned, there was, for a while, a nationally syndicated advice to-the-lovelorn column by Peggy Hopkins Joyce and then a book on her experiences *Men Marriage and Me*, as well as two novels. When she died of lung cancer, her sixth husband was at her bedside. One of her lovers explained to the author the sway she held over heterosexual males; "She went straight to the guy's ego. Peggy was easily the most orgasmic woman I've ever made love to." She is generally believed to have been the inspiration for "Lorelei Lee," one of the central figures in Anita Loos' *Gentlemen Prefer_Blondes*.

** In 2000 *Golddigger: The Outrageous Life and Times of Peggy Hopkins Joyce* by Constance Rosenblum was published.

sive collector, had saved one of the cards Jean Malin sent out for Christmas 1932, his last. It was a drawing of a handsome blond male in evening clothes, complete with top hat and cane. The salutation was what Nick Lucas had heard him use to silence the patrons that night, "Now Hear Me!!!"

One of Malin's best-known lines was quoted in at least two of his obituaries. It was an obvious reference to the Puerto Ricans and Mexicans who comprised much of the lowest paid help on both coasts: "I'd rather be *Spanish* than mannish."

By the mid-seventies I was again living in Hollywood. Billy Livingston was in the process of settling permanently in Palm Springs with a retired GM executive. Over the champagne I brought as a housewarming gift, he got talking about Jean Malin: "He was perfect for swanky joints. He knew exactly how far to go. When we met, he'd just been brought uptown to the Club Abbey from the Rubaiyat. That's where Lucas must've seen him. I was doing the costumes for the floorshow at the Abbey. One of the biggest racketeers of those days, Dutch Schultz, was there a lot and there were whispers that he was the Abbey's angel. Certainly made himself to home there because he shot it out one night just like in the gangster movies, right in the main room with another mobster named Charlie 'Chink" Sherman. Darlin', I don't know about you, but guns going off gets on my nerves. Anyway, after that The Abbey closed, but Jean was on a roll. He went right into the Argonaut, which I know for a fact was backed by Owney Madden, another big-time hoodlum. He had a partner they called 'Big Frenchy' De Mange, a name I always thought sounded positively lewd. But about Schultz. He always had two or three very pretty guys at his table. Smartly turned out. Sophisticated. The kind you like. He had goons around him, too, but they were only there as bodyguards.

"In many ways it was a better scene then. Squares didn't go to nightclubs. That started during the war years. Until '33 the drinks were illegal, the jokes were blue and the babes were spilling out of their spangles. You got married guys cheating on their wives. Rich older ladies were escorted by elegant queens or gigolos. Members of the press, socialites and celebrities, all mixed together.

"Jean sang songs such as 'There's Danger in Your Eyes, Cherie,' did imitations of stars, sometimes to their faces, and carried on like he was hosting a great party. It's about then that queens began using the word

The Ship Café alongside the Venice pier in 1910. It was to become the favorite night spot among the movie colony who would soon make Hollywood the world's film production center.

'camp.'* That's what he did, and that's what he was, a great big camp."

Usually, when I guested on radio shows that took listener call-ins, I would offer a free autographed copy of my latest book to anyone who could put me in touch with one of the celebrities of the past I had been unable to locate. In this way, I had found such personalities as Ditra Flame, the "Woman in Black" who for years made highly publicized appearances at Valentino's tomb, the World War II hero "Commando Kelly"** and Larry "Baby Dumpling" Simms, who movie fans knew from the series of twenty-eight "Blondie" features.

---

* The author's favorite explanation as to how "camp" evolved into a word meaning a special sort of humor, practiced and appreciated mainly by homosexuals, made the rounds in Manhattan shortly after Susan Sontag's "Notes on Camp" appeared. The story goes that after the Crash of 1929, large apartments in luxury Manhattan buildings became available at greatly reduced rates. Many were leased by homosexuals who then rented out rooms to others, mostly recently arrived, ambitious young men who wanted smart addresses and the company of other aspiring homosexuals of their generation. In the course of becoming acquainted an atmosphere akin to that of a chorus boys' dressing room developed. The sharing of kitchens and baths with their flat mates was though of as "camping out." Mannerisms, remarks, routines came into being that were soon known in the homosexual bars and throughout Greenwich Village as "camping." Those who did so were "camps" and described as "campy."

** Charles E. Kelly was a hero of World War II and the author of *One Man's War*. ('44).

From my point of view, the best programs were those late at night. Their audiences asked the sharpest questions and gave me the most helpful feedback.

In 1989, sometime during the wee, small hours over KABC's "Ray Briem Show," someone phoned in asking about the early career of Patsy Kelly, who had died in 1981. I told the audience that she and Ruby Keeler had been friends since adolescence and that Patsy had come into prominence as a teenager, heckling Frank Fay. Even those who disliked Fay personally, and there were many, acknowledged his mastery of timing and the quickness of his ad-libs. The dapper gent and the plump, cheeky babe played extremely well off each other.

Then, before going to the next call, I remarked that I had long sought to know all the details of the death of her friend years before. His name was Jean Malin. It was what is usually called a "freak accident" and had taken place after a show at the long gone Ship Café, a faux vessel built alongside the Venice Pier. A free, signed book to anyone...

During the next commercial break, the producer emerged from the control room and handed me a note from a listener who was present that fateful night. Furthermore, I knew her and had for years. She was profiled in my ninth book.

Thelma White was of interest to my readers for her role of the hard-bitten blonde, "Mae Coleman" hostess of marijuana parties, in the camp classic *Reefer Madness* ('36). I was to call her the following day.

I knew the name Thelma White from when I first lived in Hollywood during the fifties. During that time, she had her own talent agency. After a bout with polio, she got around mostly in a wheelchair. She shared a large comfortable house in the San Fernando Valley with Tony Millard, a show business jack-of-all-trades, whom she married in 1955.

By the time I arrived home, made myself popcorn and went to bed it was well past 4 am. When I arose, it was just after noon and there were two messages on my telephone answering machine. Fat Shelly had called to say he enjoyed the show and to advise me, "Thelma White is a lesbian, in case you didn't know." My friend and neighbor Iris Adrian wanted to tell me, "Malin was a big fag and Patsy Kelly was a dyke. So's Thelma. She wanted to handle me a few years back. Professionally, of course. I never went that route. Tell her 'hello' from Iris."

Shortly after I interviewed Thelma in 1985, I returned to view her personal copy of the 1957 TV show *This is Your Life*, with her as the surprised

Thelma White being interrogated by police in a scene from the 1935 exploitation feature, Reefer Madness. The film was intended as an expose of the pitfalls of the "Devil's Weed," marijuana.

guest of honor and one of her early clients, the actor Robert Blake. Both times I observed and sensed quite a number of subtle considerations and courtesies between the Millards. It was the sort of thoughtfulness and mutual respect that would be next to impossible to put on for company. The other thing that struck me was that Thelma's husband was obviously homosexual.

On my third visit, Mrs. Millard asked that her husband join us. He, too, wanted to know what had happened on the night of August 13, 1933. And, did I mind if she smoked.

"Depends on what you smoke," I replied through my best Gioconda smile.

After seeing the knowing and hopeful looks they exchanged, I produced a jumbo joint of Maui Wowee.

After exhaling her first drag, the lady of the house said "It's so hard for us to come by and we have to be careful. The people around us are such stick-in-the-muds."

Then, Tony nodded dreamily, "This stuff is a ...real treat."

Before her hand reached the pack of L&Ms, her husband had removed one and passed it to her. He not only lit his wife's cigarette, he liked doing it. She like his doing it. I liked watching.

A minute, or perhaps five, hard to tell when one is stoned, later, Thelma White took a sip of her iced tea. Swallowing, she let out a long, blissful sigh and asked, "Isn't this nice?"

The actress had her prop in hand and the full attention of her audience.

Thelma wasn't a bit surprised that Patsy Kelly hadn't wanted to go into what happened and why. It was so long ago and not the kind of experience anyone would want to talk about. Her good buddy had been killed, and poor Patsy was hospitalized and had her stomach pumped. It was weeks before she could go back to work. At that time, the comedienne was under contract to Hal Roach, and being coached in comedy for the camera by the veteran, Zasu Pitts.

Thelma began hearing about Jean Malin about 1927 or '28. She though all "the kids" became aware of him about that time. By "the kids" she meant the young homosexuals and lesbians who were in show business in New York City.

His real name was something unpronounceable, Polish, probably. She had heard that early on he had worked downtown in the Village in drag. Then he began to get bit parts on Broadway. One, she was pretty sure, was in *Sisters of the Chorus* ('30). But he kept getting fired for using a gesture or a look to draw attention to himself. Sometimes he said things. Things that weren't in the script. Just remarks he thought of. Of course, he got big laughs. But unless they hire you to be funny, you're not supposed to be. It throws the other actors off and the stars just will not have it. Whenever they heard Jean was going to be in something, "the kids" would run to see it before he got the boot. She couldn't swear that he originated a line that was a cliché even when she first heard it, but Jean Malin was the first one Thelma had heard use it. A woman up front during a play had a terrible coughing fit one night in the middle of a scene that was supposed to be played very quietly. Well, no one could hear the actors for her. Malin was playing the butler. Just as she had all but stopped, he swooped out on stage, looked straight at the woman and said, "*Courage*, Camille!" The house came down. Again, he was unemployed, but the word was out, "This guy's got something."

It reached the agent Lou Schwartz that there was a big blond queen named Jean Malin packing them in at the Rubaiyat. He got him a gig at

The Club New Yorker was in the basement of the Christie Hotel in the heart of Hollywood. The building is now owned and operated by Scientology.

The Abbey where he clicked overnight.

Many of the most popular entertainers of the stage and vaudeville never learned how to deal with hecklers, the bane of the nightclub business. Malin made his reputation with his gift for the big squelch.

Thelma believed she knew how he honed his art: "Jean had a boon companion, I don't think they were sweeties, just real good buddies. His name was Jimmy Forlenza. He was along that night, but got thrown clear with only a few bones broke. They'd come out to the coast together. Took an apartment up on Whitley at the La Leyenda.* After every show, Jimmy would critique it, teasing in a way, but also giving Jean all this great dialogue, 'You know what you should have said to the guy blowing all that cigar smoke?' He gave him new lines and polished some of Jean's.

"They just broke each other up all the time. Had everybody else in stitches. Jimmy should have had a career as a comedy writer."

Thelma had been brought to Hollywood to make a screen test in the early summer of 1933. When she arrived, Malin was the headliner at the Club New Yorker. It was in the basement of the Christie Hotel, which had been built by the same brothers who produced Christie Comedies during the early silent era. It was almost across from the more sedate Café Montmartre on Hollywood Boulevard. The New Yorker got a younger, faster clientele. Because of Jean Malin's reputation and the all-girl house band, Babe Eagan and Her Hollywood Redheads, they drew many of what was called "Twilight Trade."

Along with the alcohol it served, which was still illegal in California, the club offered slot machines, which were also against the law. Thelma recalled the screen funnyman Roscoe Ates, known for his stutter, juggling coins in one hand as he pulled a level over and over with the other.

The Ship Café was a replica of an old clipper. Although it had burned down even before I arrived in Los Angeles in 1952, Aileen Pringle had once shown me a postcard of the place from the twenties. The restaurant-showbar was especially popular among movie people who often came there after a day of filmmaking on the shores of the Pacific. Viola Dana, who was a star for Metro before it became part of MGM, and her sister Shirley Mason, a leading lady of the same period, remembered it as their favorite for an evening out.

Shirley, who was the younger of the two and the widow of director Sidney Lanfield, told me, "We both love boats, but get dreadfully seasick. At the Ship Café, it was just like being aboard one, except it never moved."

Malin's contact with the Club New Yorker did not include an option. When the engagement concluded, business fell off sharply. He was offered another contract with a hefty raise in salary, but his agent declined. His client had proved such a draw he deserved a cut of the cover charge as well. When the New Yorker's management balked, Schwarz booked the performer into a short run at the Ship Café to tweak their noses.

---

* 1737 N. Whitley Avenue. La Leyenda in English is "the legend."

Patsy Kelly was often where Marlin worked and Jimmy Forlenza was almost always out front or backstage. Also in the audience that night was Polly Moran, who would eventually be teamed with Patsy in two-reelers. She, like Thelma and several other names, was in attendance because it was his closing night. Afterwards, many of them planned to go into town for a private party someone was throwing at The Barn, a cavernous building on Cahuenga Boulevard that became famous during the years of World War II as the Hollywood Canteen.

Thelma's mention of The Barn was accompanied by a wink, meaning it was a bar for "the kids."

In an interview Malin gave upon arriving in Los Angeles, he complained that he had to learn to drive.

"He was a typical New Yorker," explained my hostess. "Thought all cars should come with a man and a meter in the front seat. But, like everyone, he soon realized that the city was so spread out, he had to drive. Of course, Hollywood being Hollywood, everyone gave him the routine, 'You're gonna be a star. You gotta live like one.' So, he had to have one that knocked your socks off. Had just taken delivery when he went into the Ship Café. I don't know what make it was, but it had a name, not just a brand name. A special one like 'Continental' or 'Coupe de Ville.' It was

Jean Malin's streamlined Graham Blue Streak had a straight 8 engine, hydraulic brakes, a three-speed, free-wheeling transmission and full-skirted fenders.

parked on the pier, so we all went over for a look-see before going to the parking lot for ours. I wish I could think of the model because even I'd heard of it. It was one that hasn't been made in years.

"Anyway, as we were oohing and aahing, himself and Patsy came down the gangplank with Jimmy."

"Tell him about the hood ornament," interjected her husband.

"Yes, I told Tony, thinking he might know what it was called. There was a medallion right over the grill, which was very different by the way, of the men who made the car. Not the Dodge Brothers. It wasn't a Dodge. I'd remember that. It was one that hasn't been made in years. 'Streamlined,' as we used to say. A real star's car."

My car maven, Byron Matson*, immediately recognized Thelma's description of Malin's vehicle as the Graham Blue Streak**, the official car of the 1932 Olympics. The three figures on its hood ornament represented the Graham brothers, heads of the Graham-Paige Motors Corp. of Dearborn, Michigan. Although their headgear, that of medieval knights, are different on each figure, the profile is the same. It was posed for by Tyrone Power, Sr., father of the screen matinee idol of the forties.

According to one newspaper account, the rear of the vehicle was against a safety block. Thelma remembered that to be the case and that amidst the "See you at the Barn" and "Follow us" Malin was grumbling. Something about being glad this would be the last time he would have to turn his car completely around on that narrow pier.

Thelma set the scene for us: "It was a lovely evening and not very late. There were a few people further down the pier, kids and men fishing. Maybe a couple or two watching the ocean by moonlight. Patsy had rolled down the window next to her. Big mistake. We could hear her laughing even after the motor started. Then, all at once, we heard her screams. Blood curdling and they were echoing across the water. But then she was drowned out by this terribly loud crunching noise. Something very big about to come apart. Well, everyone around started yelling and running. A lot of people said he was drunk. Impossible. He'd just come off the stage. Now Patsy was a drinker, but she wasn't driving. My hunch was that a bottle or a flask was passed around after they got

---

* Curator of the San Sylmar Auto Collection.

** The luxurious and futuristic Graham Blue Streak was advertised as "The Most Imitated Car of the year." It sold for between $1,100 and $1,295, depending on model and accessories. Among its features were hydraulic brakes, a three-speed, freewheeling transmission and full-skirted fenders. On August 13, 1932, one year to the day before Jean Malin lost his life in a Blue Streak in the Pacific Ocean, Ray Graham, youngest of the three Graham brothers, committed suicide by drowning. Tootsietoys' miniaturized version of the Blue Streak sold in the millions and are now collector's items.

in the car. Just as the swig Jean took hit him, the car slammed against the safety block and he panicked. Stepped on the gas instead of the brakes. We'll never know, will we? You can guess what happened next. That big, beautiful new car went right off the pier backwards. Big crash. Huge splash.

One of the guys who flew out of the Ship Café to see what was going on was a lifeguard. Off came his shoes and coat and in he dove. They were in fairly shallow water, but the car had turned over in the fall, so all that dirty water was pouring in on poor Patsy.

"I heard later that Jean was killed on impact, and I hope and pray that's true. Being such a big guy, they couldn't get him out from behind the steering wheel.

"The police and the fire department were there lickety-split, and Patsy was taken away with sirens screaming. I'll never forget the way she looked when they brought her up. I didn't expect her to pull through, but thank God, she did. Jimmy was hurt, but nothing serious. Funny, I never heard tell of him since that awful night. Whatever became of Jimmy Forlenza? That's a case for Richard Lamparski. Isn't it?"

John Robbins and several friends were having a nightcap in the Ship Café when they heard the commotion outside. He lingered on the Venice pier after the taillights of the rescue unit and squad cars disappeared into the darkness.

"When they were gone, it became very still," he told me over that dinner in 1971. "All you could hear was the surf below slapping against the pilings. Less than an hour before he'd had us howling. I think when he walked on stage at his final show and saw Polly Moran at one of the front tables, he just pulled out all stops. All the queens loved her. Sudden death stuns you. I was twenty-two. Malin was twenty-four. We, maybe four or five of us all about the same age, just stood there staring at each other. No one knew what to say. Then one of the boys glanced in the ocean where the car had crashed and said, 'Oh, God! Look!'

"We could see the Ship Café's poster announcing his appearance reflected in the dark waters. There was a blinking bulb illuminating the small sign beneath it.

"What we saw was:
JEAN MALIN and then
Last Nite…
Last Nite…
Last Nite…"

My All-Time Favorite Hollywood Story

By the late sixties, there were movie clubs in New York, Hollywood and San Francisco. One of the first was Bob Chatterton's Parlour Cinema. In the living room of his low-ceilinged two-bedroom apartment in North Hollywood, he held regular showings of films most of us hadn't seen since childhood, if ever. You had to be recommended to join, seats had to be reserved in advance and you were responsible for the behavior of anyone you brought. I usually took someone along, always taking care to explain beforehand the rules: No smoking. No talking once the projector begins to roll, and no comments that could be considered criticism or ridicule, no matter what was on the screen. Use the john before or after each feature only. Place two dollars in the cigar box by the door.

Women were welcome and there was always at least one present, the host's ninety-some-year old mother. On most nights, just before the show began, Mrs. Chatterton, who got about on a four-pronged cane, shooed their trio of dachshunds into her bedroom where she watched TV wearing earphones. The only times she joined us was if Bob ran a Deanna Durbin film and whenever he was able to secure a print of a Ruth Chatterton picture.

There were two things the Chattertons wanted all Parlour Cinema newcomers to know right off. One was that they were related to the screen and stage star. She had always visited them whenever she came to Cleveland, their hometown, in a play back in the thirties and forties. Bob's father had been her first cousin. According to his son, many of the Chatterton family ostracized the actress after they learned she was "living in sin" at some point with the Broadway producer, Gilbert Miller.

The other was that in the parking lot on the left of the building where they had lived for years once stood the home of the former world's heavyweight boxing champion Jack Dempsey. He had lived there with the hot-eyed dramatic actress Estelle Taylor during their marriage.

When I came across a souvenir postcard from the twenties of that house I gave it to the Chattertons for Christmas. They carried on and on about it, had it framed and hung it proudly in their bathroom.

One evening, I took as my guest Anselma Dell'Olio, who as an arch feminist was beginning to view the tearjerkers of the thirties as primary sources in the conditioning of women, themselves as well as their mothers. I had introduced her to the work of a few other queens of the genre, such as Helen Twelvetrees, Constance Bennett and Gladys George, when I first knew her in New York.

The feature at the Parlour Cinema that night was *Female* ('33) in which Ruth Chatterton gladly exchanged the directorship of an automobile works she owns for marriage to her chief engineer, George Brent, her husband in real life. Anselma had been with me only a few months before when I interviewed Brent in La Jolla. That she had met the definitive leading man of his time made her all the more anxious to see this typical woman's picture of the Great Depression.

One thing I didn't prepare her for, because I didn't know how, was the intensity of feeling held by most of the old-movie buffs about their favorites. Many of them were fans since childhood of certain personalities and had never wavered in their devotion over the years in which their pictures were not available for viewing. Such types were all but contemptuous of those who were just then being introduced to the classics of the silents and early talkies. They had absolutely no patience for naïve questions such as "Who's he?" and "Is *this* the star?"

Sometimes I would encounter film historians and biographers, such as DeWitt Bodeen and Charles Higham, at these showings, but very few of the regulars were professionals and the majority had about them the blandness of manner and appearance one associates with clerical workers. They were not, however, lacking in temperament and were quick to flare if anyone dared to challenge the reputation of one of *their* stars.

One night as the lights went on at the end of DeMille's version of *Cleopatra* ('34), a woman remarked innocently that she was going the next day to the Saturday Matinee to purchase some portraits of Claudette Colbert, who played the title role. Sitting in front of her was the former president and longtime pillar of the Alice Faye Appreciation Society, next to Ian, his housemate who hung a life-size oil painting of his favorite, the character actress Edna May Oliver, in their kitchen.

The former turned around and said, "You really only need one. Colbert looked exactly the same in every picture." The woman, who was a newcomer and didn't know him, was somewhat taken aback, but said nothing.

He then popped into the bathroom. By the time he came out, his words had been repeated throughout the room and drew the ire of a male couple who in tandem unleashed such fury the three dogs began barking.

Chatterton had to intervene with, "Please settle all that outside, boys."

Even after Bob closed the front door behind them, we could make out the cries of "Big moo-cow eyes!" and "Old picklepuss" from the street.

When I introduced Anselma to the Chattertons, she said something about never having heard of Ruth Chatterton until she had met me and had yet to see any of her films. After we took our seats, a fortyish male in front of us turned around. He could have doubled for the comedic character actor Franklin Pangborn. Obviously, he had overhead the Dell Olio's remark of moments before. He waited until we settled to proclaim, "Ruth Chatterton *was* the 'First Lady of the Talkies,' a *major* stage star and was *twice** nominated for an Academy Award." That said, his head and shoulder turned from us as though on a well-oiled swivel. So there.

Once in a great while, a star would be in the audience at the Parlour Cinema to see for the first time in many years, and in some cases ever, one of his or her own pictures. Most insisted their presence not be announced beforehand. Mae Clarke came to see a rare and very clear print of *Waterloo Bridge* ('31), believed by her admirers to be superior to the Vivien Leigh re-make.

"Judy Canova in person!" heralded the club's monthly flyer when she agreed to attend a double bill of "B" starrers she made at Republic Studios, *Puddin' Head* ('41) and *Joan of Ozark* ('42). The only proviso she insisted upon was that "That Richard Lamparski not be on the premises." Several years before, I had guested on radio station KDKA Pittsburgh, my last stop before returning home after a long, exhausting publicity tour. The first listener to phone in asked, "There was a comedienne back in the forties. For a while she had a radio program. Made movies, too. Always played hicks or hillbillies. Her name was Judy Canova. Can you tell me what she's doing these days?"

---

* For *Madam X* Ruth Chatterton was nominated as the Best Actress of 1929-30 and again in 1930-31 for *Sarah and Son*.

It was just past 9 PM (EST). I replied, "In California where she lives, it's early evening, so Judy's probably either out in her front yard, feeding the chickens or around back, slopping the hogs."

One of her fans was recording the broadcast and sent her an audio tape.

I had no right to make that or any other rude remark. Because of it, I never got to meet Judy Canova, and I would have liked to. Looking to the brighter side of the incident, however, it delighted quite a number of people to know I had been banned from her personal appearance. It also gave them a story to tell and re-tell whenever either of our names was mentioned for years to come. From what I understand, my uncalled for and completely untrue quip was repeated, as well. It, I'm told, got a big laugh.

My next trip to the West Coast was at Christmastime, 1970. A day or two after my arrival, Bob Chatterton phoned to tell me of something that had recently occurred when he showed *Meet Me in St. Louis* ('44). Someone had brought with him the actor Tom Drake, who arrived early and then sequestered himself in Bob's bedroom until just before the picture went on. Then, Drake and the member took seats in the last row. When the lights went on 113 minutes later and the dozen or so others in attendance recognized the man about whom Judy Garland had just sung "The Boy Next Door," he was at first applauded and then fawned over.

By then, Drake was used to being asked in such situations, not about his career or well-being, but endless questions about "Judy". There were those who remembered that, as one of Hollywood's "most eligible bachelors" of the forties, he had been engaged to Jack Haley's daughter, Gloria.*

Everyone enjoyed the movie and Tom reveled in all the attention. It was a big night for the fiftyish actor who was then supporting himself by selling used cars in the lot directly across from the entrance to MGM studios. There was, however, one of that audience who remained silent. He followed Drake and his companion out to their car. Just as the latter was unlocking its door, he said, '*You* are Tom Drake! I would never have recognized you from what we saw tonight or *The Green Years* or *Words and Music*. What *happened* to you?"

The encounter, Chatterton told me, staggered Drake, who remained leery of fans for the remainder of his life.

When Bob concluded telling me about the incident he said, "What about if I told Tom that you want to put him in one of your books? He needs an ego boost just now."

---

* The widow and daughter of Jack Haley co-hosted the repast held for Tom Drake after his funeral in 1982.

Tom Drake, during all the years I knew him, never stopped trying for a come-back and yet, from what I observed, his attitude and every move worked against him. Our first meeting, at his request, took place in Dolores's Drive-In on Wilshire Blvd. In the forties it was a popular hangout for the "Young Hollywood" set of which he had once been part. I remembered seeing a photo of Lon McCallister on a date with June Haver taken at Dolores's in a fan magazine when I was in junior high school and wondered whether Drake and I were now seated in the same booth.

To humor the actor, I ordered one of the house specialties, Boston cream pie, which I found less than special. When I saw the amount of sugar he put into each of the many cups of black coffee he drank, I strongly suspected he was "on the program," as Alcoholics Anonymous members call it.

He sometimes referred to his former studio as "Metro" and at other times it was "MGM." Now and then he gave it the full "Metro-Goldwyn-Mayer." Although he acted in pictures long after his option there was dropped, the years he spent at the Culver City lot had been, both professionally and personally, the apex of his life.

During that interview on January 6, 1971, Drake allowed that he was still getting his hair cuts at the barbershop at his old studio. I found this statement doubly awkward, because it called attention to what was obvious to begin with, his toupee.

He once told me, and I have had others say almost exactly the same words, "To be under contract to MGM was not just being in movies. You were appearing in Metro-Goldwyn-Mayer movies."

His inflection was such that one could tell it made Tom Drake feel better just by saying those words.

Anyone who sat on a folding chair at the Parlour Cinema was obliged to collapse and return it to the corner before leaving. It made the evenings that much easier for our host who had a pronounced limp; the result of a polio attack during his childhood. It had worsened as he approached sixty, due partially to his weight, which was at least twice what his height and frame were meant to carry. Bob continued, however, to look after himself, his aged mother and their dogs. Another challenge was his lifelong addiction to sweets, which played havoc with the diabetes that manifested itself in later years.

I never heard Chatterton complain about anything. The announcements and descriptions he wrote in his flyers and the out-going messages on his answering machine were always upbeat, if a bit corny. He obviously enjoyed his club and took real pride in how many newcomers had discovered films of the past or came to appreciate particular players in his living room.

To escape the dog days of summer in Manhattan, I usually spent a month in Los Angeles. Near the end of my stay in August, 1971, Bob phoned to say that one of his members wanted to meet me. It was Robert Osborne, the author of the annual *Academy Awards Illustrated*, books I used frequently in my work. At this point in his career he was editing an in-flight magazine for an airline.

Osborne asked me to lunch at the Egg and the Eye, a restaurant specializing in omelettes across from the Los Angeles County Museum of Art. Even in a city known for good-looking people, Osborne stood out for his thick, prematurely white hair setting off young leading-man features.

I believe he intended to ask me to write *Whatever Became of...?* features on a regular basis for his publication. I, however, must have said something that made him reconsider, because he made no such offer. I may have let it slip that I had neither a favorite star nor picture. Somehow Robert Osborne caught on that I was not one of his kind, a member of the Hollywood establishment or even a movie buff.

Our conversation became rather stilted. Then he asked whom I had interviewed lately. It was the perfect opening to change the mood that had set in about our table and to share the best story I'd been told in some time.

Beulah Bondi's unofficial, but undisputed title was "Queen of the Character Actresses." She was as admired within her profession as among moviegoers.

When I mentioned to Louise Brooks that I had an appointment to meet with Ms. Bondi in her home, it triggered a recall of Bondi's performance in Elmer Rice's *Street Scene*. She had seen it shortly after it opened on Broadway in 1929.

I knew from reading the play that its set was the facades of a block of turn-of-the-century Manhattan brownstones and that it took place during a heat wave.

Louise remembered how Bondi, who played a building's superintendent, at one point was discovered backing down the front stoop as she swept. She continued slowly until she reached the curb. Then, leaning on her broom as though she was about to keel over, she wiped her brow with a bare forearm. After a long deep sigh, she reached wearily around behind her and pulled the thin, tattered dress that clung to her from the crack in her ass.

"Darling," she exclaimed over thirty years after the experience, "That gesture was felt throughout the theatre. With it, she told us it was such a scorcher that she wasn't wearing panties. I said to myself, '*This* is some actress!'"

I concluded my account of the interview with Beulah Bondi by telling Osborne its highlight. For me, a writer, that is. It pained my hostess to repeat the experience. One of the questions I ask almost all of my interviewees is, "Was there a role that you wanted with all your heart that somehow slipped by?"

For Ms. Bondi, there had been two. The first she actually got and was then replaced through no fault of hers.

Shortly after David O. Selznick announced that May Robson would play Aunt Polly in his production of *The Adventures of Tom Sawyer* ('38), the actress became so ill she had to withdraw. Beulah was signed in her stead and the picture had just begun shooting when, to her own as well as her doctor's astonishment, Miss Robson made a quick, complete recovery. There was nothing embarrassing about the switch because she had stepped in for the original choice who was now available. It was completely understandable and there was an upside to the affair because she was paid her full salary for a few days' work.

The other, however, was quite another matter. Never had there been a screen assignment she had wanted more than that of Ma Joad in *The Grapes of Wrath* ('40). She and just about every other character actress in the United States of America. It was the role of a lifetime. When her agent told her its director, John Ford, had thought of her all the time he was reading the script, they both felt she stood a very good chance. After all, during the four years since the Academy of Motion Pictures Arts and Sciences had been awarding supporting actresses Oscars, Beulah Bondi had been nominated twice, the first year of the category, for *The Gorgeous Hussy* and in 1938 for *Of Human Hearts*.

In preparation for the screen test, she made several discreet, incognito visits to some of the very encampments of Okies John Steinbeck wrote of in his 1939 Pulitzer Prize winning novel. Disguised in threadbare clothes, she managed for a while to move among the migrants unnoticed, listening to speech patterns and watching body language. After one of the inhabitants remarked that she had seen Beulah "Someplace before," she never returned.

As Ms. Bondi explained over three decades later, "Those poor souls had enough to contend with. Knowing that an actress was studying them would have been just too cruel."

Then she told about what happened on the first day she went to Orange Country and roamed about a camp like Steinbeck had described. A woman aged beyond her years from a poor diet and a life of hardship emerged from one of the tarpaper shacks proclaiming "The good Lord be praised!" As others gathered around her, she shared the good news. Her daughter-in-law had just given birth to her first grandson. Beulah engaged her in conversation and was asked inside to meet the mother and see the brand new baby.

"Here they were," she said. "Without electricity or running water. It was a hovel with a dirt floor and no pane in the one window. But, I'll never forget the pride with which I was shown that infant. He was the future of their family and both of those women were positively joyous over him."

She then paused for a moment and swallowed. The remembering had upset her.

"Well, when I turned to leave I saw what someone had printed over the entryway in big letters, 'We Are Grateful.' I sat in my car for the longest time afterwards. I couldn't drive, you see, because of the way I was crying."

When I suggested that tears would have been out of character for Ma Joad she quickly agreed, "You are absolutely right, Richard, I would *never* have done it for the screen."

When Beulah Bondi left the set after making her screen test, John Ford walked her to the door of the soundstage, telling her that as far as he was concerned, she had created the Ma Joad he had in mind. She had never learned what had happened after reading in *Daily Variety* that the role had gone to Jane Darwell.

Robert Osborne never let on what he knew until later. He just sat there eating his coconut cream pie as I went on about the beautiful Bondi home* in Whitley Heights. In its walled courtyard was a small statue of St. Francis of Assisi. The Spanish Colonial structure had been built into

---

* The house at 6660 Whitley Terrace had been the home of Joseph Schildkraut, the first recipient of the Best Supporting Actor Oscar for the role of Captain Alfred Dreyfuss in *The Life of Emile Zola* which was chosen Best Picture of 1937. Beulah Bondi bought the property from the parents of Sybil Jason, child star of the thirties.

the hillside during the twenties and featured a sunken living room with a beamed cathedral ceiling. In the circular dining room on the upper story, the actress entertained her contemporaries.

Ann Doran told me she knew she had been accepted by her peers the first time Miss Bondi included her at one of the luncheons she hosted.

"There were at least a dozen of us," she recalled. "Here I was a California gal seated between Aline MacMahon and Anne Revere, with Gale Sondergaard directly across from me. *All* from the Broadway stage, but we got on like a house on fire. The thing that floored me was the way Beulah had the table set. Every plate was fine china, Rosenthal, Spode, what have you. Each was of a different pattern and color. I never saw that done before or since. The effect was quite beautiful, by the way."

Osborne knew what had happened between the director's encouraging comment and the final casting because Jane Darwell had told him. When he first arrived in Hollywood, an aspiring actor, he had rented a small cottage on her property, part of what had once been a small farm in Van Nuys. The actress had no children, but enjoyed and to a great extent understood young people, especially those who were striving for an acting career. As Osborne put it, "Jane grandmothered Jane Withers in five of

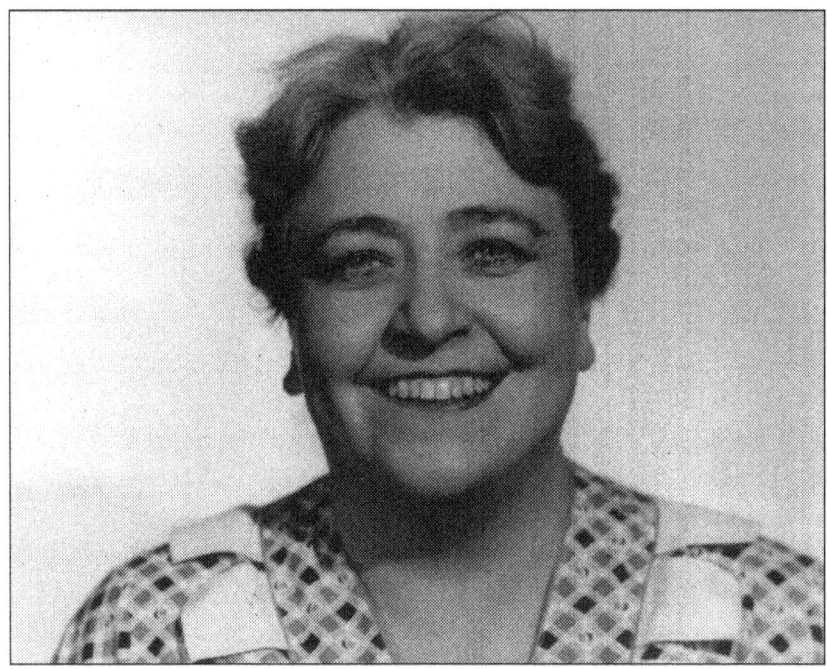

Jane Darwell nursed the Dionne quintuplets, supported Shirley Temple and grandmothered Jane Withers at Fox Films until her contract was allowed to expire in 1938.

her starrers and supported Shirley Temple in similar roles in six of hers. She knew kids all wanted to sit in her lap."

I had always thought of Jane Darwell's lap as second only to my own grandmother's. Those pictures as well as *Five of a Kind* ('38) in which she played nurse to the Dionne Quintuplets were all made at Fox Films, where she had been pacted in 1934. Exactly four years later, the day before her contract was up for renewal, Miss Darwell received a telegram at her house at 5450 Ethel Ave. advising her that the studio was not going to exercise its option on her services. No reason was given.

Jane Darwell had trained and toured for years with the Morosco Players, a stock company that then included Lewis Stone, who became best known to movie goers as Judge Hardy, the father in the Hardy Family series. Wesley Ruggles, who became a director, as well as his actor brother Charlie, were also members.

She was used to being assigned roles, not "going after" them, as it's called in Hollywood. But, even before the screen rights to *The Grapes of Wrath* had been purchased by Twentieth Century-Fox, as her former studio was now called, Jane had read it and had her heart set on playing Ma Joad. She knew the odds were against her because Darryl F. Zanuck, the head of production, was the same man who had let her go the year before.

Her agent could not talk the casting director into even letting her make a screen test. His efforts drew the comment, "*No one* on that picture can see your client in the part."

Her next step was impolitic bordering on the foolhardy. She made several phone calls to the studio head's office. When none were returned, Jane Darwell drove to her old lot and sat patiently in his outer office. Cautioned by his executive secretary that being confronted might anger him, she replied that she needed only one minute of his time. Whenever he emerged, she would walk with him to the elevator pleading her case.

Hours later, Darryl F. Zanuck, brandishing his trademark riding crop exited his office. The moment he saw the stout actress he said, "Look, Jane, I know why you're here. I'm going to be blunt. The woman you're seeking to portray is half-starving. How are you going to *act* that?"

Producers are renowned for not reading properties, they pay fortunes to film. It was a gamble Miss Darwell had counted on, and she played her trump card by opening the copy of the book she was holding and read aloud: "Ma was heavy, but not fat; thick from child-bearing and work."

The flunkies and secretaries around him held their breaths. Proving D.F.Z. wrong in front of his staff was all but unthinkable. And yet, there it was in front of him in black and white, just as Steinbeck had written it.

"Well, I still don't think you're right for it, but go ahead and test," was his terse decision.

Jane arrived early in the morning, although her test was not scheduled until 11 AM. After being made-up, she slipped into a dress she found at the Salvation Army outlet that fit the description the author gave of Ma's costume: "A loose Mother Hubbard of gray cloth in which there had once been colored flowers, but the cloth was washed out now, so that the small flowered pattern was only a little lighter gray than the background."

The screen tests were being directed by John Ford. At 1 PM when he dismissed his company for lunch, Jane was still waiting. They would reconvene at 2:30, but she had no appetite. Rather than just sitting around waiting, she drove around the city, worrying, fulminating, working herself up even more than she had been.

But then, as she told her tenant years later, "Something kinda wonderful happened. The thought came to me that the state I was in was what Ma's must have been all the time. She had to have felt unwanted and mistreated. She must have been scared like I was. But she couldn't let it show. She had to be strong enough for her whole family. It was almost time to go back to Fox. By then I *was* hungry. Good. I'd make the camera see that, too."

The first thing she was told by the assistant director was that she wouldn't be needed for at least another hour. Moments later, she overheard a script supervisor tell someone, "It's Beulah Bondi by a mile. Mr. Ford almost applauded when she finished."

At 4:30 when she finally walked onto the set, Jane Darwell was looking every day of her sixty-some years. She was bone-tired and felt more than a bit insulted. After being one of the first actresses to arrive, she was the very last to be called. As her key light was being adjusted, Henry Fonda who was on his mark across from her smiled and wished her luck. Then she heard Ford's assistant call, "Quiet on the set!"

As soon as Jane Darwell pulled her car around the back of the house that evening, her three St. Bernards started barking. It was at least an hour past their usual mealtime. Her nephew Winston, who boarded with her, had just gotten in from work. He began scooping out their feed as his aunt plopped herself down at the kitchen table.

So, how had the test gone?

It had felt good. She was tuckered out, but she felt good.

"Funny thing," said Jane. "Seconds before the camera began to roll my stomach growled."

"*That*", opined Winston Ogden, "Was Ma Joad letting you know she was with you."

Weeks went by before the news broke in the trade papers that Jane Darwell had been chosen for the much-coveted role of Ma Joad.

In the 1974 book *The Western Films of John Ford* its author, Janey Ann Place, explained the rightness of the casting: "The soil would have hardened Beulah Bondi; it regenerates Jane Darwell. Its depletion would have impoverished the former, while the latter seems sustained by her physical and spiritual abundance. Darwell is like a mound of earth, solid and warm."

It was her nephew who filled in the detail for me of how his aunt got the part that brought her the Best Supporting Actress Oscar for 1940. By then, it was 1973 and Jane Darwell had been dead for six years.

Alfred Lunt and Lynn Fontaine, generally considered at the time to be the first couple of the American theatre, presented Jane Darwell and Walter Brennan with their Best Supporting Oscars.

Jane Darwell and Henry Fonda in a scene from The Grapes of Wrath *(1940).*

The Oscar Jane Darwell received was in the form of a plaque. It was not until 1943 that Best Supporting actors were given statuettes.

Winston Ogden was bed-ridden and in obvious discomfort. Despite extreme shortness of breath, he seemed to relish the telling of how the producer, director and star of *The Grapes of Wrath* all watched the screen tests for the first time together. Zanuck, who sat in the last row, questioned Ford and both took and made phone calls throughout. The only performance to draw his full attention was Beulah Bondi's.

"That's it!" was the boss's pronouncement. "Who's gonna best that?"

One of the honored adages of the film capital is that no one knows what the camera has captured until it is viewed *on the screen*.

Both John Ford and Henry Fonda remained seated when their producer stood to leave. Professional courtesy dictated that they at least see the remaining footage. Zanuck, however, would have left the screening room then if he hadn't received a call that lasted through several more tests. Hanging up, he stepped into the aisle as the projectionist called out, "Just one more, Mr. Zanuck. It's Jane Darwell."

"*Forget* Jane Darwell," was the firm response.

Turning back to him from the front row, the director said, "She made the effort, Darryl. Why don't we at least have a look at what she did?" With that the lights dimmed and the images of Henry Fonda and Jane Darwell came onto the screen. When they came up again, the three sat it total silence. Slowly, the director and the actor turned back toward Zanuck, but they waited for him to speak.

"*Both* of you?" the producer asked.

"That's Ma," said one. "*Has* to be," said the other.

"So be it," remarked the studio head, tersely.

As the trio with Zanuck in the lead headed up the stairs to the exit, a young man stepped out of the projection booth carrying cans of film.

"Wait a minute," said his employer. "How is it we saw Jane Darwell last?" It was asked with all the authority of a Hollywood mogul, a somewhat suspicious one.

"She tested last, Mr. Zanuck," was his reply. True, but…

It was a few years before Jane learned about how and why on that day she came to be the closing act, so to speak, an actress's dream. At the wrap party for one of the three subsequent pictures Miss Darwell was to make under John Ford's direction, her nephew thought it was *My Darling Clementine* ('46), someone told the story.

That projectionist had come to Fox Films directly from high school and worked first as an errand boy on its Western Avenue lot. Coming from a small Midwestern town, he felt intimidated just being at a movie studio and was tongue-tied around the famous personalities and high-powered executives.

Just before lunch one day, he was sent with a script revision to Jane Darwell's dressing room. She complimented him on the sweater he was wearing and they ended up sharing her sandwich and fruit. Whenever he visited the actress after that, she helped him to overcome his shyness. He sought her advice, came to think of her as a friend.

"That was just like Jane," Ogden recalled. "She was always encouraging me, saying things that built my confidence. He had to have been rooting for her to land such a plum role."

The Oscar her nephew had inherited from his aunt was proudly displayed on his bureau. As it was being photographed, he told me that a few years before she died the Academy of Motion Pictures Arts and Sciences offered to exchange the plaque she received for one of the statuettes known around the world.

"Aunt Jane wouldn't have traded hers for anything," he assured me. "It matched the one in that picture." He was pointing to the framed photograph on the wall. In it Jane, wearing a spray of orchids, is standing alongside fellow recipient Walter Brennan. They had just been presented their awards by the unofficial first couple of the American stage, Alfred Lunt and Lynn Fontanne, who are on the left.

As I prepared to leave Winston Ogden asked me the title of whatever it was I was writing. I didn't have one, but the notes I had taken along with the photos of Jane Darwell's Academy Award went into my file labeled "My All-Time Favorite Hollywood Story."

Index

"After You've Gone"	66	Andrews Sistaers	77
"Boy Next Door, The"	98	Anger, Kenneth	16
"Broadway Rose"	2	*Annie Get Your Gun*	86
"Camp"	138	Arbuckle, Roscoe "Fatty"	13, 19
"Frankie and Johnny"	67	*Arizona to Broadway*	134
"Little Annie Fanny"	62	Ates, Roscoe	143
"Mad About the Boy"	54		
"Moondog" (Louis Hardin)	2	Balance, Bill	116
"There's a Small Hotel"	15	Bankhead, Tallulah	59, 128-9
"There's Danger In Your Eyes, Cherie"	137	Banky, Vilma	106, 113
"Thin Man. The"	126	Barn, The	144
"Tip Toe Through the Tulips"	132	Barrett, Rona	65
		Barry Sisters	77
Abbey, The	61, 137	Barry, Joan	8
Academy Award	94	Baruch, Bernard	67
Academy Awards Ills.	152	Basquette, Lina	126
Academy of Motion Pictures, Arts and Sciences	51, 52, 53	Baum, Vicki	98
Acquanetta	33, 34, 35, 132	Beard, Mathew "Stymie"	27, 32, 34, 35
Adams, Evangeline	3	*Beau Geste*	95
Adams, Nick	53	Beck, Thomas	102
Adler, Polly	134	*Becoming Mae West*	68
Adrian	40	Beery, Wallace	13
Adrian, Iris	23, 139	Behan, Brenden	69
Adventures of Tom Sawyer	153	Bel Air Fire	95
AFTRA	42	*Bell, Book and Candle*	44
Albertson, Chris	1	Bennett, Constance	148
Alcoholic Anonymous	43, 151	Bennett, Joan	134
Alexander, Ron	86	Benny, Jack	4
Alice Faye Appreciation Soc.	148	Bergner, Elisabeth	103
Alyn, Kirk	34	Besser, Joe	27, 33
AM San Francisco	85	Beverly Hills Hotel	74, 117
Amateau, Rod	49	Beverly Wilshire Hotel	115
		Blake, Robert	140

Blue Angel, The	108, 112	Chatterton, Bob	147, 149
Boardman, Eleanor	9	Chatterton, Ruth	10, 65, 147, 148, 149
Bodeen, DeWitt	14, 15, 101, 102, 113, 148	Cherrill, Virginia	136
Bogart, Humphrey	7	Christi, Frank	5, 6, 27
Bondi, Beulah	152, 153, 154, 157, 160	Christian, Linda	72
		Christie, Hotel	132, 142
Boswell Sisters	77	*Christine Jorgensen Story, The*	53
Bow, Clara	99, 109	*Cimarron City*	116
Bowers, John	92, 93, 95	Ciro's	59
Boyer, Charles	53	Clarke, Mae	149
Brand, Harry	66	Clive, Henry	132
Brand, Sybil	66	Club Abbey	137
Brennan, Jim	37-50	Club New Yorker	132, 142, 143
Brennan, Walter	158	Cock 'n Bull	108
Brent, George	10, 148	Cocteau, Jean	16, 109
Brooks, Louise	61, 62, 65, 103, 152, 157	Cohn, Harry	9
		Cohn, Roy	65
Brown, Johnny Mack	13	Colbert, Claudette	131-2, 148-9
Browning, Tod	8	Collyer Brothers	15
Buckskin	85	*Constant Sinner, The*	61
Buckwheat	35	Conte, Ruth	120, 121
Bullocks Wilshire	104	Cooper, Gary	6, 8, 95, 99, 110, 111
Burnett, Carole	47	Copage, Marc	85
Burr, Raymond	110	Cornell, Katherine	99
		Coward, Noël	102
Campton Place Hotel	85	Crabbe "Buster" Larry	13
Canova, Judy	66, 149, 150	Crawford, Joan	7, 21, 65, 110, 134
Cantor, Ida (Mrs. Eddie)	98	Cresendo, The	72
Captain Midnight	38	Crisp, Quentin	1-24
Carr, Alan	9	Criswell	66
Carroll, Diahann	85	Cromwell, Richard	97-112, 106
Carson, Johnny	66	Crosby, Bing	4
Carson, Robert E.	94-6	Cypress Hills Cemetery	57
Carson, Sunset	32		
Carter, Jimmy	22	D'Heilly, Jean-Louis	25
Catherine the Great	69	Damita, Lily	9
Cavanaugh, Paul	65	Dana, Viola	143
Central Casting	62	*Dancing Lady*	134
Chaney, Lon Sr.	9	Dangerfield, Rodney	74
Chapin, Lauren	33, 84	Darwell, Jane	147-161
Chaplin, Charles	8, 13, 26, 117	Davies, Marion	9, 19
Chasen, Maud	22	Davis Bette	21, 59, 69, 99, 101, 107
Chasen's	21, 41		
Chateau Marmont	86	Davis, Buster	128

Davis, Sammy Jr.	63
Davis, Shelly "Fat"	71-80, 139
Day, Doris	49, 77
De La Motte, Marguerite	92, 93, 95
DeBrier, Samson	16, 17, 136
Decker, John	22
DeHaven, Gloria	54, 71
Dell'Olio, Anselma	148, 149
DeMange, "Big Frenchie"	137
DeMarco Sisters	77
DeMille, Cecil B.	13, 19, 110, 125, 148
Dempsey, Jack	133, 148
Di Frazzo, Dorothy	110
Dietrich, Marlene	9, 59, 107
Diller, Phyllis	72
Dionne Quintuplets	155-6
Disney, Walt	116
Donahue, Troy	115
Donohue, Jimmy	134
Doran, Ann	155
Drake, Christopher	100-113
Drake, Tom	98, 150, 151
Dressler, Marie	109
Du Brey, Claire	99
Duck Soup	78
Duke, Doris	9, 105
Dumpling, Baby	71, 73, 80, 104
Duna, Steffi	54, 55, 56
Dunhill, Ford	115
Dunne, Dominick	127
Durbin, Deana	147
Eagan, Babe and Her Hollywood Redheads	143
Eagels, Jeanne	101
Eason, Jim	97
Eells, George	16, 61, 62, 63, 72, 134
Eilers, Sally	16
Emma	109
Eternal Grind, The	94
Fairbanks, Douglas, Sr.	92
Falcon, Lair	8, 75, 105, 106
Father Knows Best	84
Fay, Frank	11, 139
Faye, Alice	4
Faye, Frances	38
Fellini, Frederico	69
Female	148
Fields, W.C.	21, 22, 59, 99, 129
Filmarte Theatre	14, 17
Five of a Kind	156
Flame and the Flesh	45
Flamé Ditra	138
Flynn Errol	9
Fonda, Henry	109, 160
Fontaine, Lynn	158
Forbes, Ralph	10
Ford, Films of John	158
Ford, John	153, 157, 160
Forest Lawn, Glendale	65
Forlenza, Jimmy	142, 144, 145
Forman, Milos	3
Frascati's	115
Freaks	8, 127
Friendly Persuasion	115
Gable, Clark	7, 110
Galli-Curci, Amelita	98
Garbo, Greta	99
Garland, Judy	59, 98, 150
Gassman, Vittorio	9
Gates, Phyllis	121
Gaynor, Janet	15
Gentry, Race	115
George, Gladys	148
Gibson, Hoot	16, 17
Gilbert, John	94
Gish, Lillian	94
Givot, George	69
Glassner, Lester	23, 24
Gleason, Jackie	11
Gleason, James	126
Gleason, Lucille	126
Gleason, Russell	126
Glyn, Elinor	125
Go West, Young Man	59

Goddard, Paulette	8
Godowsky, Dagmar	126
Goebbels, Joseph Dr.	99, 104, 107
Gold Diggers of Broadway	132
Gold, Sam	66
Goodman, Benny	30
Goodrich, Bert	66
Gorgeous Hussy	153
Graham Blue Streak	144
Graham-Paige	145
Grand Hotel	98
Grant, Cary	12, 136
Grapes of Wrath, The	147-161
Gray, Billy	85
Greatest Show on Earth, The	53
Green Years, The	150
Grey, Lita	8
Griffith, Corinne	94
Guinan, "Texas"	17, 132
Haines, William	113
Haley, Jack and Flo	131, 150
Hall, Alexander	131
Hamer, Rusty	87, 88, 89
Hamilton, George	8
Hamilton, Neil	100
Hammett, Dashiel	126
Harlem	62
Harris, Phil	4, 5
Hart, Lorenz	12, 13, 15
Hatton, Raymond	13
Hatton, Rondo	125
Hayworth, Rita	74
Head, Edith	66
Hearst, William Randolph	19, 58
Hedda and Louella	134
Henie, Sonja	76
Henreid, Paul	53
Henry, Buck	3
Hi Diddle Diddle	106
High and Mighty, The	115
Higham, Charles	148
Hilton, Hotel, Beverly Hills	99
His Hour	125
Hoffman, Dustin	33

Holden, William	50
Holiday, Billie	38
Hollywood Canteen	144
Hollywood Roosevelt	46
Hood, Darla	20, 25-36
Hooded Falcon, The	106
Hoopla	109
Hovey, Tim	85
Hudson, Mrs. Rock	121
Hudson, Rock	47-50, 115
Hunter, Ross	66
Hunter, Tab	115
Ice Capades	52, 59, 76
Interlude, The	38, 72
Iron Mask, The	94
Irving, Mary Jane	94-6
It's a Gift	21
Jackson, Marty	117-121
Jason, Sybil	26, 154
Jealousy	101
Jessel, George	20
Jezebel	109
Joan of Ozark	149
Joan of Paris	53
John Birch Society	126
Johns, Glynis	98
Jones, Buck	13
Joy	64, 67
Joy, Leatrice	94, 126
Joyce, Peggy Hopkins	136
Julia	85
KABC, Radio	139
Karl, Harry	74
KDKA Radio	149
Kean, Betty	129, 130
Kean, Jane	129
Keaton, Buster	13, 20
Keeler, Ruby	128
Kelley, Kitty	74
Kelly, "Commando" Charles	138
Kelly, Patsy	11, 128, 129, 130, 139, 144, 145

Index 167

Kelton, Pert	11, 13	Livingston, Billy	59, 76, 102, 129, 132, 136, 137
Kennedy, John F.	10		
Kenyon, Doris	106	Lloyd, Harold	101
Kerry, Norman	94	Logan, Jacqueline	125
KFMB, San Diego	115	Lonergan, Wayne	127, 128
KGO-Radio	97	Long Beach Pike	110
KGO-TV	85	*Lorna Doone*	94
King of Kings	125	Lowe, Edmund	9
Kirkwood, James	131	Loy, Myrna	96
Klaw, Paula	123, 124, 125	Lucas, Nick	137
Koll, Don	128	Lunt, Alfred	158
Kosleck, Martin	100-113		
Kreuger, Kurt	109	*M*A*S*H*	91
KUSC-FM	89	Mack, Helen	9
		MacKaill, Dorothy	94
Lahr, Bert	130	MacMahon, Aline	155
Lake, Arthur	27, 33	*Mad Doctor, The*	104
Lamas, Fernando	45	Madden, Owney	61, 137
LaMirada Theatre	14	Mafia	65
Lamour, Dorothy	38	Maine, Hotel	94
Lancaster, Burt	99	Malin, Jean	129-146
Lanfield, Sidney	143	Malin, Lucille	134, 136
Lanier Margie	5	Malone, Dorothy	53
Lansbury, Angela	104	*Man on the Flying Trapeze*	21
Laramie	120	Mansfield, Jayne	63
LaRocque, Rod	113	Mapes, Jacques	66
LaRue, Jack	32	Marais, Jean	108
LaRue, Lash	13	March, Fredric	93, 94
Lassie	83, 84, 87, 88	Marion, Frances	113
LaVey, Anton	62, 104	Marmon	94
LaVey, Diana	62	Marx Bothers, The	78
LaVey, Stanton	62, 104, 105, 107	Marx, Gummo	77, 80
LaVey, Zeena	62, 63, 65, 104	Marx, Zeppo	77, 77-80
Leach, Archie (Cary Grant)	12	*Mask of Zorro, The*	94
Lear, Norman	53	Mason, Shirley	143
Lee, Gypsy Rose	76	Massey, Raymond	39
Lee, Lila	131	Matson, Byron	145
Leider, Emily Wortis	68	Maugham, William Somerset	101
Leigh, Janet	43	McBean, Angus	1, 2
Leigh, Vivien	149	McCalla, Irish	27
Letter, The	101	McCallister, Lon	102, 151
Leyenda, La	143	McCarthy, Charlie	57
Liberace	42, 47, 130	McNair, Barbara	63
Lillie, Bea	99	McQueen, Steve	47
Lives of a Bengal Lancer	111	*Meet Me in St. Louis*	98, 150

Mendelssohn, Eleanora von	103, 108, 109
Mendelssohn, Felix	103
Menjou, Adolphe	19, 106
Merman, Ethel	61
Millard, Tony	139, 140
Miller, Gilbert	147
Miller, Mark	49
Miller, Patsy Ruth	2, 106, 126
Mineo, Sal	10
Miracle Mile, The	96
Miss Lonely Hearts	126
Miss Ohio	119
Mix, Tom	17
Moffat, Ivan	74
Monroe, Marilyn	84
Monroe, Michael	98
Monti, Carlotta	21
Moore, Terry	98, 121
Moran, Polly	144
Morosco Players	156
Movie Star News	123, 126
Mr. America of 1939	66
Murray, James	9
Murray, Ken	27
Muscle Beach	60
Musgrove, Stanley	47, 59, 60, 62, 63
Music For Airports	89
Musso & Frank's Grill	85
My Darling Clementine	160
My Little Chickadee	59
Myers, Carmel	106
Nader, George	49
Nadler, Reggie	40
Naked Civil Servant, The	1, 5, 22
Nebel, "Long" John	128
Negri, Pola	8, 106
Nesbit, Evelyn	98
No, No, Nanette	128, 130
Nobel, John	1, 2
Nolan, Tom	85
Novak, Paul	60, 65-69
O'Brien, George	15, 16
O'Brien, Virginia	32

O'Day, Anita	61, 72, 73
O'Donohue, Joseph J. IV	134
O'Keefe, Dennis	54, 55, 56
O'Neill, Oona	8
Of Human Hearts	153
Ogden, Winston	157, 158, 160, 161
Oliver, Edna May	149
On Your Toes	15
Orden, Robert Van	115
Original Joe's	128
Orry-Kelly	11
Osborne, Robert	147, 152, 153, 154
Oscar's Wine Bar	65, 86
Page, Betty	62, 123
Palm, The	45
Palmer, Lilli	44-5
Pangborn, Franklin	149
Parker, Dorothy	126
Parsons, Louella O.	110
Pasternak, Joseph	39
Patten, Luana	116, 117, 120
Payne, John	53-56, 71
Peck, Gregory	21
Pendleton, Jimmy	40
Perino's	96
Pickens Sisters	77
Pickfair	8, 117
Pickford, Mary	94
Place, Janey Ann	158
Pleasure Man	61, 63
Polish National Catholic Church	1
Poppy	99
Porcel	71
Porter, Cole	61, 99
Powell, William	96
Power, Tyrone, Jr.	19
Power, Tyrone, Mrs.	72
Power, Tyrone, Sr.	145
Preminger, Otto	107
Preston, Robert	98
Pringle, Aileen	103, 125, 143
Puddin' Head	149
Pulitzer Prize	153
Pupi's	40

Putnam, Opal	109, 110
Pyne, Joe	71
Raft, George	76, 95
Randall, Jack	13
Randall, Tony	49
Rappe, Virginia	19
Rathbone, Basil	104
Ravenswood, The	61
Ray Breim Show, The	139
Ray, Johnnie	38
Ray, Man	95
Raye, Martha	72
Reagan, Ronald	21
Reefer Madness	139
Rettig, Tommy	27, 32, 33, 83-89
Revere, Anne	155
Revier, Dorothy	106
Reynolds, Debbie	74
Rice, Elmer	152
Richardson, Sara	25, 26
Righter, Carol	2
Ringling Bros. and Barnum & Bailey Circus	76
Ritz Brothers	77
River of No Return	84
Roach, Hal Sr.	29
Robbins, John	124, 126, 127, 128, 134, 145
Robbins, Tod	126
Roberti, Lyda	130
Roberts, Clete	91-96
Robinson, Edw. Jr.	119
Robson, May	153
Rodgers, Richard	12, 15
Rogers, Buddy	8
Rohmer, Sax	1
Romanoff's	7
Roosevelt, Eleanor	67, 68
Rubaiyat, The	137, 141
Rubin, Cyma	128
Ruby Gentry	44
Ruggles, Charles	156
Ruggles, Wesley	156

Saks Fifth Avenue	96
Sales, Soupy	71-80
Salisbury, Monroe	13
San Sylmar Auto Collection	145
Sandy, Baby	32, 33, 138
Satanic Bible, The	62
Scandia	41
Schaefer, Natalie	63
Schenck, Joseph	20
Schultz, Dutch	137
Schwab's Pharmacy	40, 77, 78, 133
Schwartz, F.A.O.	104
Schwartz, Lou	141, 143
Searle, Jackie	97
Selznick, David O.	94, 153
Seven Little Foys, The	77
Sextette	65
Sharpe, Karen	115
Shaw, Artie	30, 31
She Done Him Wrong	59
Shearer, Norma	9
Sherman, Charlie "Chink"	137
Shields, Jimmy	113
Ship Café, The	138, 139, 143, 144, 145
Shirley, Anne	6, 54
Siam, King and Queen of	8
Siegel, Benjamin "Bugsy"	71
Sinatra, Frank	7, 77, 78
Sinclair, Upton	98
Sisters of the Chorus	141
Skolsky, Sidney	133, 134
Smiley, Allen	71
Smith, Bessie	1
Smith, John	115-121
Sondergaard, Gale	155
Sondheim, "Foxie"	3
Sondheim, Stephen	3
Song To Remember, A	99
Sontag, Susan	138
Sothern, Ann	110
Souls at Sea	95
St. John, Al "Fuzzy"	13
St. Joseph, Ellis	51
St. Moritz, Hotel	77

Stanwyck, Barbara	54
Star Is Born, A (1954)	115
Star Is Born, A (1937)	91-96
Steele, Bob	13
Stein, Gertrude	61
Steinbeck, John	153, 154, 157
Stevenson, Venetia	121
Stone, Lewis	156
Street Scene	152
Stricklyn, Ray	27, 33, 34, 35, 102
Stroheim, Erich von	50, 59
Sunday, Billy	133
Sunrise	15
Sunset Boulevard	50
Sunset Tower	41, 77, 78, 80, 102
Sutton East Hotel	125, 126
Swanson, Gloria	11, 50
Taft, Robert A.	29
Talmadge, Constance	20, 133
Talmadge, Natalie	20
Talmadge, Norma	20
Taras Bulba	53
Tashman, Lilyan	9, 110
Taylor, Elizabeth	29
Taylor, Estelle	148
Taylor, Richard	5
Taylor, Robert	54, 55, 56
Taylor, Ruth	2, 3
Temple, Shirley	155-6
Thalberg, Irving	9
There Really Was a Hollywood	43
Thiess, Ursula	54, 55
This Day and Age	110
This Is Your Life	139
Thomas, Danny	87
Thomas, Kevin	66
Thompson, Carlos	45
Three Musketeers, The	94
Three Stooges, The	77
Three Weeks	125
Todd, Thelma	130
Tol'able David	99
Tone, Franchot	111
Torch Singer	132
Toulouse-Lautrec	85
Tucker, Lorenzo	61
Tucker, Sophie	72
Turner, Lana	30, 31, 45, 53
Tuttles of Tahiti	95
Twelvetrees, Helen	148
Two Mrs. Carrolls, The	103
Valentino, Rudolph	75, 105, 106, 138
Variety	45
Velez, Lupe	8, 111
Vidor, King	9
Villa Madrid	98
Wales, Prince of	8
Wanamaker, Marc	132
War of the Worlds	57
Warner-Kelton Hotel	11, 12, 13, 14, 15, 17
Washington, Dinah	38
Waterloo Bridge	149
Wayne, John	41, 53
Webb, Clifton	20
Webb, Maybelle	20
Weiss, Harry Esq.	65
Welles, Orson	57
Wellman, William	94
West, Beverly	67, 69
West, Mae	47, 57-69, 129
West, Nathanael	87, 126
Western Union	95
Weston, Ray Dr.	74
Whalen, Michael	102
Whatever Became Of...?	40, 46, 85, 95, 100, 115, 128, 152
Whatever Happened To Baby Jane?	21
Whiskey a Go-Go	71
White Shoulders	75, 76
White, Thelma	139, 140, 141
Wholey, Dennis	27
Wilder, Billy	108
Will Rogers State Beach	38
Williams, Emlyn	1

Williams, Tennessee	19, 130
Willingham, Calder	3
Willson, Henry	115
Wilson, Lois	126
Wilson, Lois	94, 106, 126
Windeler, Robert	54
Wise, Robert	59
Withers Jane	155
Woman Commands, A	106
World's Fair in 1940	127
Wyndham, Hotel	131
Young Mr. Lincoln	109
Zanuck, Darryl F.	156, 157, 160
Zucco, George	51

BearManorMedia

P O Box 750 * Boalsburg, PA 16827

Hollywood's Golden Age
by Edward Dmytryk
$17.95   ISBN: 0-9714570-4-2

A legend remembers the good old days of films...Edward Dmytryk, director of The Caine Mutiny, Murder, My Sweet, Hitler's Children and a host of other classic movies, has written a powerful memoir of his early days in Hollywood. From peeking in at the special effects for The Ten Commandmants, the original silent film, to his first job as an editor, slowly, patiently splicing film...Dmytryk's brilliantly written and until now unpublished look back on old Hollywood is a joy you won't be able to put down.

My Fifteen Minutes
An Autobiography of a Warner Brothers Child Star
by Sybil Jason $18.95   1-59393-023-2

Sybil Jason was Warner Brothers' first child star. Friend of Humphrey Bogart, Roddy McDowall, Freddie Bartholomew, Shirley Temple and dozens of other Hollywood stars, her fan club is still international. Her captivating story is enriched with over 100 rare photos from her personal collection.

A Funny Thing Happened on the Way to the Honeymooners...I Had a Life
by Jane Kean
$17.95   ISBN: 0-9714570-9-3

Jane Kean's frank and funny memoirs of a show business life are a loving first-hand account of what it was like growing up among the Who's Who of classic Hollywood and Broadway. She tells all—and tells it like it was. From starring stage roles in *Early to Bed*, *Call Me Mister*, and *Ankles Aweigh*, to such presitigious films as Disney's *Pete's Dragon*, Ms. Kean has lived the show biz life. Having performed extensively with her comical sister Betty, Jane is perhaps best known as Trixie in the award-winning television series, *The Honeymooners*.

visit www.bearmanormedia.com
Visa & Mastercard accepted. Add $2.50 postage per book.

BearManorMedia
P O Box 750 * Boalsburg, PA 16827

Plain Beautiful:
The Life of Peggy Ann Garner

The life story of one of Hollywood's most beloved child actors, whose performance in *A Tree Grows in Brooklyn* won her the Oscar.

$19.95   ISBN 1-59393-017-8

Spotlights & Shadows
The Albert Salmi Story

You know the face. You know the credit list: *Lost in Space, Escape from the Planet of the Apes, Gunsmoke, Bonanza, Kung Fu, The Twilight Zone* and hundreds more…But who was Albert Salmi?

Sandra Grabman's biography is a frank and loving tribute, combined with many memories from Salmi's family, friends, and co-stars, and includes never-before-published memoirs from the man himself. From humble beginnings—to a highly successful acting career—to a tragic death that shocked the world—Albert Salmi's story is unlike any other you'll ever read.

$19.95   ISBN: 1-59393-001-1

visit www.bearmanormedia.com
Visa & Mastercard accepted. Add $2.50 postage per book.

CHECK THESE TITLES! BearManorMedia.com

P O Box 750 * Boalsburg, PA 16827

Comic Strips and Comic Books of Radio's Golden Age
by Ron Lackmann

From Archie Andrews to Tom Mix, all radio characters and programs that ever stemmed from a comic book or comic strip in radio's golden age are collected here, for the first time, in an easy-to-read, A through Z book by Ron Lackmann!

$19.95 ISBN 1-59393-021-6

The Old-Time Radio Trivia Book
by Mel Simons

Test your OTR knowledge with the ultimate radio trivia book, compiled by long-time radio personality & interviewer, Mel Simons. The book is liberally illustrated with photos of radio stars from the author's personal collection.

$14.95 ISBN 1-59393-022-4

How Underdog Was Born
by creators Buck Biggers & Chet Stover

The creators of Total Television, the brains behind Underdog, Tennessee Tuxedo and many classic cartoons, reveal the origin of one of cartoon's greatest champions—Underdog! From conception to worldwide megahit, the entire story of the birth of Total Television at last closes an important gap in animated television history.

$19.95 ISBN 1-59393-025-9

Perverse, Adverse and Rottenverse
by June Foray

June Foray, voice of Rocky the Flying Squirrel and Natasha on Rocky and Bullwinkle, has assembled a hilarious collection of humorous essays aimed at knocking the hats off conventions and conventional sayings. Her highly literate work is reminiscent of John Lennon, S.J. Pearlman, with a smattering of P.G. Wodehouse's love of language. This is the first book from the voice of Warner Brothers' Grandma (Tweety cartoons) and Stan Freberg's favorite gal!

$14.95 ISBN 1-59393-020-8

The Writings of Paul Frees

A full-length screenplay (The Demon from Dimension X!), TV treatments and songs written for Spike Jones— never before published rarities. First 500 copies come with a free CD of unreleased Frees goodies!

$19.95 ISBN 1-59393-011-9

Daws Butler – Characters Actor
by Ben Ohmart and Joe Bevilacqua

The official biography of the voice of Yogi Bear, Huckleberry Hound and all things Hanna-Barbera. This first book on master voice actor Daws Butler has been assembled through personal scrapbooks, letters and intimate interviews with family and co-workers. Foreword by Daws' most famous student, Nancy Cartwright (the voice of Bart Simpson).

$24.95 ISBN 1-59393-015-1

For all these books and more, visit www.bearmanormedia.com or write info@ritzbros.com
Visa & Mastercard accepted. Add $2.50 postage per book.

BearManorMedia
P O Box 750 * Boalsburg, PA 16827

I Love the Illusion
The Life and Career of Agnes Moorehead
by Charles Transberg
$19.95

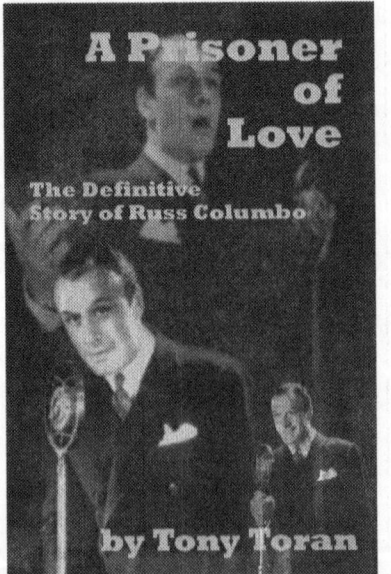

A Prisoner of Love
The Definitive Story of Russ Columbo
by Tony Toran
$29.95

Please add $3.00 postage per book.

BearManorMedia
P O Box 750 * Boalsburg, PA 16827

Hold That Joan
The Life, Laughs and Films of Joan Davis
by Ben Ohmart
$24.95

Talking To the Piano Player
Silent Film Stars, Writers and Directors Remember
by Stuart Oderman
$19.95

Please add $2.50 postage per book.

BearManorMedia
P O Box 750 * Boalsburg, PA 16827

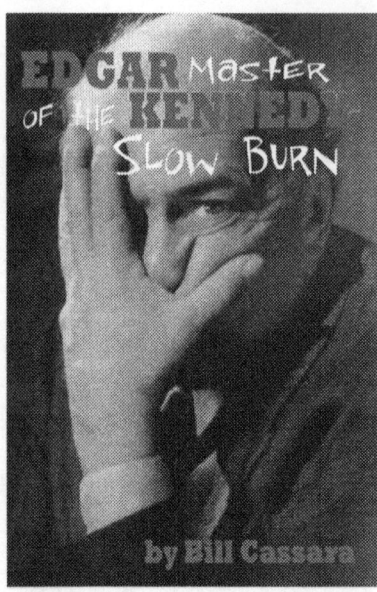

Master of the Slow Burn

by Bill Cassara

$19.95

A Leonard Maltin pick!
They Started Talking

by Frank Tuttle

Edited & with an Introduction by John Franceschina

$19.95

Please add $2.50 postage per book.

BearManorMedia

P O Box 750 * Boalsburg, PA 16827

The Man Behind the Mask

by Antoinette Girgenti Lane

$29.95

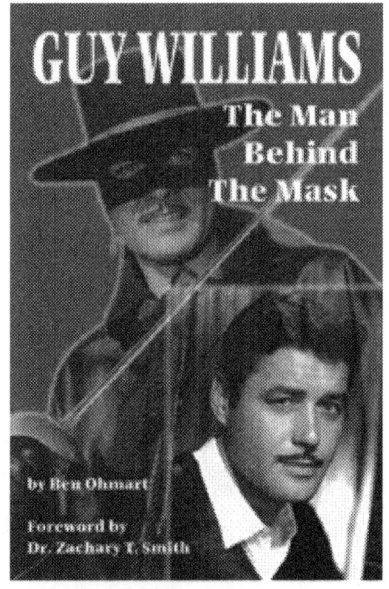

Nothing Lost Forever
The Films of Tom Schiller

by Michael Streeter

$16.95

Please add $2.50 postage per book.

BearManorMedia
P O Box 750 * Boalsburg, PA 16827

The Old-Time Radio Trivia Book

by Mel Simons

$14.95

The Old-Time Television Trivia Book

by Mel Simons

$14.95

Please add $2.50 postage per book.

Coming soon from
BearManorMedia
P O Box 750 * Boalsburg, PA 16827

Manhattan Diary

by Richard Lamparski

Peggy Lee, Truman Capote, Christine Jorgensen, Lenny Bruce, Lynn Bari, Tallulah Bankhead, Dorothy Parker, Fannie Hurst, Dagmar Godowsky, Sammy Kaye, Joan Bennett

and

"The Greatest Star of Them All!"

www.ingramcontent.com/pod-product-compliance
Lightning Source LLC
Chambersburg PA
CBHW022102160426
43198CB00008B/322